To Cla
My f
with affection

THE WIND
ALSO LISTENS

Alvin Cummins

caribbeanchapters

First Edition. September, 2008

Edited and Published by
Caribbean Chapters, P.O. Box 4133
Speightstown, St. Peter, Barbados
www.caribbeanchapters.com

Note for Librarians:
A cataloguing record for this book is available
from the Barbados Public Library

Send questions or comments to:
caribbeanchapters@gmail.com

ISBN:
978-976-8219-10-7
paperback

Foreword

It is a natural human inclination to escape from uncomfortable or confining places or situations. The social atmosphere, poverty, prejudice, low wages and lack of opportunity existing in Barbados in the 1950s and early 1960s was so stifling and stultifying that many of the inhabitants of the island tried to escape by whatever means they could.

Unless history is recorded, coming generations will be unaware of what preceded them. Barbados' advancement in all spheres since the late 1960s is due in large measure to the 'exiles' who escaped the society of earlier times; the 'exiles' whose cries were heard by the wind which listened and transmitted their cries until relief was obtained. Part of that relief is the recording of the events of an earlier time, in this work motivated by the desire to enlighten future generations on earlier society's actions and attitudes, and their consequences.

'The Wind Also Listens' looks at the lives of six young people who sought to escape by varying means from the circumstances that affected their lives. Although from different backgrounds, they are all equally affected by the societal attitudes which keep them imprisoned. One of them cannot escape from the social stigma of his lifestyle and seeks death to end his imprisonment.

Mothers in this matriarchal society have always functioned as a source of strength, comfort and guidance, and their roles in shaping the lives of the heroes and heroines of the society are explored in this book.

****

Dedicated to my two daughters Carolyn and Charlene, to my sisters Jean and Beverley, and to all those who consider themselves 'exiles'

Prologue

You never knew me; who I was,
and am, and always will be.
You never could see inside,
to see the love there was,
and is, and always will be.
I am what I am,
and what I am, and who I am,—
was pre-ordained by One
far greater than you or I.
Soon I will be no more,
and when I'm gone, by then you'll know
who I was, and what I could have been, with you.
But now, I am alone beside the lake,
and my voice echoes in this cold, deserted land
silent, except for the wind; the wind which listens
to my voice, crying
In Exile.

PART I

The Beginning

Harpur

You awaken slowly. It is very early in the morning. You become aware of your surroundings equally slowly. You sit up on your bed and look outside your window, and everything you see is new and unfamiliar.

Trees; a forest of them; an army of dark sentinels; tall, sturdy, straight, with arms bereft of leaves, greet your eyesight. The air is sharp and crisp, bearing scents unplaced, odors unrecognized. A white man is digging a ditch. He is fat and dirty. The pickaxe swings up and down without rhythm. Sweat drips from his forehead and he pulls a dirty red cloth from his dirty jeans and wipes his dirty face. Another one is shoveling the dirt into a wheelbarrow. He also is dirty, fat, and sweaty. A third one carts away the dirt to add to the growing pile at the side of the path which will eventually become a road.

You are shaken. A white man digging ditches? A white man shoveling dirt? A white man working hard? How could this be? White people never did these things where you came from; where you were born.

Your gaze shifts past the pine trees stretching into the distance to where the moving vehicles seem like an endless column of ants in some urgent and unending quest. It is all strange and new.

A snore jerks your attention back to your room, and once more reinforces the strangeness of your surroundings, and the longing for home washes over you in waves like the surf over the shelving sands of the beaches back home. Another man is in the room, a white man. You don't take much notice of his features.

Nostalgia engulfs you, and you fight the tears which try to force themselves to the surface. You long for a familiar face; a smell of home. A dawn, a rising sun in a sky of shifting colors; a sea shimmering silver, ruffled by a breeze, gentle, soothing, bringing with its touch a promise. Home. The patient sighing of casuarinas, while the woman tongues* keep up their ceaseless chatter and talk with the wind which listens and answers with its breath, caressing the ripening arrows of the sugar cane. And the sea, a canvas of changing colors. Blue green, aquamarine, black. Roaring surf, and spray, salty, sharp, good to taste. Peace and quiet. Home.

There is the sound of a bus rumbling and rattling in the distance, its engine's scream faint as it winds its way up the steep hills which meander to the sea, passing among the green foliage of the sugar cane stalks and the trees. The bark of an awakened dog echoing from somewhere in the distance. The air is cool and soothing. Buxom, laughing women with buckets of water on their heads, walking seductively, gracefully. Laughing, playing children with skillets at the pipe where everyone in the village gets their water to fill the tubs, and to give to the animals before going to school. The village is coming awake. Home.

The memory of the little school in the front room of the two bedroom house where you were born impinges on your consciousness. You see the back room with its single bed and dresser, your parents' only possessions, where you breathed that first breath which gave you life, but set you on the inevitable path... to death?

But for that first breath you would not now be experiencing this loneliness, this longing, this yearning for home. And the memories come flooding back.

You see Wellington Street, where you were born. It is cut, slashed, disemboweled by Nelson Street, the main street of the slum area. The alleys which branch off from it are narrow and chock full of 'low islanders', immigrants from St. Lucia, Dominica, or one of the other islands. Jessamy Lane, Queen Street, Duke's Street, all alleys where a man rubbed shoulders with each wall as he passed between the houses on either side. Where nostrils are assaulted by the smell of urine—days-old in coconut shells—from countless diseased, crab-loused, semen-stale penises; rotten mangoes, rotten oranges, and rotten garbage.

Rooms with smut lamps, bottles with cloth tightly rolled for a wick and fuelled by kerosene. Crocus bag beds, lice, bedbugs, dirt. Toilets without doors in narrow yards divided by pieces of board or tin, put on in a crazy pattern, which allow more to be seen than hidden. Toilets with buckets to shit in. This is Nelson Street. Shit is what Nelson Street is—a hole; a dungeon. Some lived and had their being, and died, in Nelson Street. Some got their clap* and passed it on in Nelson Street.

In Jordan's Lane, crazy-mixed-up, dirty houses lean wearily against each other, seeking comfort and solace by overlapping windows. At night the air is pungent with the smell of frying fish or fray cakes* from half a dozen frying pans on coal pots glowing red in the dark doorways of half a dozen shops.

Cheap perfume on stinking bodies. Myriad odors from different sources. Clashing sounds of music. Different sounds and songs from different hotels and bars, all loud, all harsh. God! What a place!

The scene shifts and you see when you take your first toddling steps. You are attracted by the sound of children learning, singing, and growing in the school, learning by repetition:

> *Twice ones are two, two into two one.*
> *Twice twos are four, two into four two.*
> *Twice threes are six, two into six three.*
> *One and one are two,*
> *Two and two are four,*
> *Four and four are eight*

7

And the hymn, always the same, or so it seemed:

> *There is a green hill far away,*
> *Without a city wall,*
> *Where the dear Lord was crucified,*
> *Who died to save us all.*

It was a hymn that you heard and sang many times throughout your elementary and secondary school years.

Mrs. G. must have been at least sixty years old when you came into the world and added to the noise in the main school with your cries. She was short and thin, and had a small, dark, wrinkled face upon which sat a pair of gold framed glasses. She kept a few fowls in the yard which constantly came into the front-house* where the classes were conducted, and messed on the floor and benches. She used to keep the sick chicks in her bosom to give them warmth even while she was teaching. She taught all the classes, from toddlers to those who were preparing to enter primary school. She also gave piano lessons. Did she ever get paid for them?

The years pass and you are soon in those same classes reciting the tables and standing on the bench for some childish misdemeanor. She is gone now, and the chickens have left her yard.

You are soon enrolled in Wesley Hall Boy's elementary school. Wesley Hall means many things to you. It is pride in the school, pride in the school song, which stays with you even today:

> *Dear Wesley Hall we love thee....*

Wesley Hall is fights in the line where you have to stand for inspection before classes to ensure that clothes are tidy, shoes shined and hair combed; it is bruises, cuts, milk and biscuits, and molasses during the war years. It is discipline and learning.

Lashes for spelling mistakes, and lashes for arithmetic and dirty finger nails. It is races around the 'marl hole' where the garbage from the classrooms is dumped. It is running out of the classrooms during simulated air-raid drills, and climbing the star-apple tree* and not finding any, and playing 'Tarzan' in the clammy cherry* trees and sticking book leaves* with the clammy cherries. It is scraping desks at the end of term with slivers of glass picked up from the garbage boxes at the door of the hardware store in Roebuck Street while on the way to school. It is the stillness of a deserted school yard on a Saturday morning before private lessons, with money your mother could not afford. It is green mangoes, water-holes with tadpoles, messing yourself before you can get to the toilet, and watching others work in the carpentry shop while you must stick to your writing. It is never getting to play in the 'big' games because you are too small, and contributing your pennies to the Empire Day* collections, and singing:

> *Rule Britannia, Britannia rules the waves,*
> *And Britons never, never, never, shall be slaves.*

Waterloo Alley is another disease-ridden artery coming off from Wellington Street. It is only about a hundred yards long, beginning in Wellington Street and ending in Bay Street. Or perhaps it began in Bay Street. However you look at it, it is the same. It has always been the home of pimps, prostitutes, and those denizens of the dark who feel like having a change from Nelson street. It is also a very convenient place for whores to call at and catch a sailor passing along Bay Street, and bring him for a few quick 'jooks', a clutch, an exchange of coins, and probably a dose of gonorrhea.

The houses, inanimate imitations of their occupants, lean tiredly on each other, seemingly in sorrow and distress. Dirty rags hang from doors and windows, and sometimes serve to divide a single room into a bedroom and living/dining room-kitchen. The rooms are papered with yellowed newspapers, bits of magazines and posters, forming a meaningless collage; abstract mirror images of their occupants.

A canal, or rather a deep gutter, passes on the outskirts behind the public bath and toilets, forming an unintentional boundary. Its water, thick and stinking, slowly moves toward its outlet and escapes into the sea. The bitches, long tits hanging from their emaciated bodies, lie unmoving on the hot tar. They too are sick like their owners.

Your grandfather is a shoemaker. His house is in Waterloo Alley.

You are too young to be aware of or understand the tension that must have existed between your mother and your aunts, but there must have been something. Maybe there were too many being accommodated in the tiny home, which made living together unbearable. It may have had something to do with the children, for it was only later, as you grew, that you realized how ferociously protective your mother was.

Whatever it was, the abruptness of her response showed the depth of her resolve and independent nature.

Your mother wakes you,

"Come. We can't stay here any longer."

"But it is dark, so dark."

"We have to find some place to go tonight. Aunt Viv does not want us here anymore."

And with the bundles and your sister and brother, you leave Waterloo Alley, its filth, vice and degradation.

Foxes have holes and the birds their nests, but the son of man has nowhere to lay his weary head. GOD! GOD! WHERE ARE YOU? TO HELL WITH YOU!

You spent the rest of the night at the Central Police Station where the kindly sergeant provided accommodation until the sun rose, and then helped her find a room to rent in Halls Road, just over the bakery, in a house near Belmont Road, a decent neighbourhood at the time.

Other memories come, not as a constant stream of unbroken film from the recesses of your subconscious, but as disjointed remembrances, disjointed like the glass slides of the magic lantern* projections of *The Pilgrim's Progress* that your mother took you to see at St. Ambrose church as part of your early childhood upbringing, each slide representing an episode in Pilgrim's upward path to salvation; each slide of your remembrances an episode indelibly etched in your memory bank and recalled spontaneously to bring comfort in your loneliness.

These silken threads of remembrance that come so early on this morning, in this strange place with unaccustomed faces, calm the panic that wants to overwhelm you. The strands of familiar events and persons envelop you like a cocoon, and warm you, and you remember.

PART II

Remembrances

Clement

It is from the window of the small chattel house as a child that you first see the sea of black, angry heads on bodies carrying sticks and knives and cutlasses, looking for white men to chop up. Black men filled with anticipation, poised for RIOT!!! All doors and windows are closed and bolted, and few people dare look out.

What is it all about?

You only begin to understand after you are a man that this is the beginning of the end. The emancipation of the Bajan Black man. The end of a dynasty and colonial overlords. The end of political domination, but not economic domination. That stranglehold remains. It tightens, even today. When will it ever end? Or will it ever?

The morning is warm. The crowd before the courthouse in Coleridge Street is steadily growing. Suttle Street is disgorging the inhabitants who lodge in its maw. A murmur fills the air, a breeze bringing a message destined to drive away the vapors clouding their minds.

From all corners of Bridgetown they come. Men, hands roughened from pulling the spiders—hand carts which carried the puncheons of molasses—and the ten-foot sweeps* on lighters*, moving between the careenage and the steamships bringing cargo to the island. Men out of work now, and women too.

"Look de van coming."

"Where it is?"

"Look it coming 'round the corner."

"Make room let it pass."

"Man stop shoving nuh! You want to shove me under the wheels?"

The black van drives inside the gates and comes to a halt. The crowd presses closer to get a glimpse of the prisoner. This is the 'Minister of Propaganda'. As he pushes his head out of the van and into the sunshine, blinking at the glare after the darkness of the van, he smiles and waves to his followers. The smile lasts only a short while though, the muscles of the strong jaw tighten.

The policemen holding him roughly jerk him around and push him toward the cellar that leads to the cells under the courthouse.

"If they lock he up it is bare trouble 'bout here. I tell you."

"He can't get lock up man. He is the shepherd come to lead us to the promised land."

"I going to make sure and carry my whomper* with me tonight, and I going be in the forefront if those white people try to make trouble. Today going be a funny night."

Long after he disappears from their sight the crowd still mills around in the courtyard. Some sit under the trees across the road, some squat on the sidewalks or shelter from the hot sun under the verandas of the nearby houses.

He has held them spellbound with his speeches. They listen and absorb as the desert absorbs the rain. They listen and ponder. They return to Golden Square time and time again to hear a new gospel, a gospel of emancipation. They hear his words and believe them. They believe him. They believe in him.

"My brothers and sisters, I have come back to the land of my birth to bring a new message. My mission is to improve the method of living and procedures of organization in this land of ours. For too long have we suffered and slaved for the white man. For too long have we tolerated and endured all that he has thrown at us. For too long we heard the voices of our children, our beautiful, beloved Black children crying to us in their hunger, and we have nothing to give them. The time has come, my brethren, for us to take action against those who hang the millstone around our necks, and make us the foot stools of their feet. They have controlled our destiny, our lives, and even our souls, from the time they tore us from the dark breast of Mother Africa. They took us, princes, and the sons and daughters of princes, and gave us only suffering.

It is time we controlled our own destiny. They say we are free, that there is no longer slavery. But we are only free to be hungry. We are still slaves to the plantation and to the Roebuck Street merchants when we never have enough money to pay them. I say all this must change. We must exterminate those who stand between us and those who keep us in bondage. The middle-class, those whimpering rabbits, unable to act according to their own conscience through fear of the white man, must go. Progress must not be halted. Do not be afraid of those red-striped, helmeted servants of the capitalists, for they too will be buried under the surging tide of progress."

"But I don't understan' what he saying."

"Never mind, his mouth sweet and the words does flow like syrup when a syrup barrel bust, so he must be know what he saying."

Another voice joins in.

"What he say make sense, because I does work hard twelve hours a day for a spaugie* red man, an' I does only get four shillings when the week come. I can't even buy a little milk to put in the children tea on a morning. I only able to get a half pound of pork every other Sunday to give the rice taste. These times hard, hard, an I can't stand it much longer."

An angry voice breaks into their discussion.

"Looka, why the hell you don't shut wunna mouths and let people hear what the man got to say?"

The conversation stops and the voice of the 'Minister' keeps up its loud harangue. It is after eleven o'clock. The night is

17

hot, the air still, hushed, waiting. The leaves of the trees also wait, unmoving. There is no wind to talk to them. The wind is listening.

Payne's loud voice still continues, untiringly. As he promised before he entered the courthouse that morning, he speaks to them. The upturned faces are intent, serious, unsmiling as they listen. He is drawing to a close and his anxious followers hear:

"Tomorrow we will form a procession and march to Government House to protest these harsh conditions and this fine levied against me. Are you with me?"

"YES! YES!" Their voices rise like thunderous, roaring surf rushing to the shore at Bathsheba.

The sun rises slowly the next day.

It is morning and as he and his followers make their way to Government House, the crowd swells as the procession passes each street, alley, or gap.

"I wish to have an interview with the governor!" Payne is at the head of the milling crowd.

The white officer, resplendent in his fine leather boots, shiny leather belt, ribbons across the chest of his khaki suit, and his 'rod of authority' under his arm, draws himself erect, a cynical smile playing around the corners of his lips.

"You will have to arrange an interview through the governor's private secretary."

The policemen are drawn up in two ranks of ten behind him. Each one carries a rifle. The smile grows slightly wider, but his eyes, flashing blue in the morning sunlight, show the hate which burns within him. 'Carrion,' he thinks. 'Dirty smelly carrion.'

"White man, I want to see his Excellency." Payne's voice rises in its insistence.

"I have already told you how you may see him."

The crowd murmurs. The wind listens. The breeze blows.

"Come on now. You will have to disperse and leave this area. Come on, MOVE!"

The breeze rustles through the trees and the leaves nod in reply. The crowd shifts restlessly and murmurs, but it doesn't leave.

"Disperse I say!"

The officer is getting angrier. How dare these Black men refuse to obey his orders? From whom do they suddenly get the courage to stand up to a white man and not cower when his voice is raised? Before, they had always jumped and hastened to obey his every word. He turns to the policemen.

"Disperse this crowd."

The tree tops sway and the branches bend. The wind is stronger now. With batons rising and falling without rhythm, the policemen burst into the crowd.

"Arrest that man!"

The officer's voice can be heard above the din. There is a sparkle of glee in his eyes as he watches the scene of confusion before him from the side. Black against Black.

His arrest is inevitable. He is a threat to the system.

He is brought into the courtroom. He places his hand on the Bible and swears to 'tell the truth, the whole truth and nothing but the truth, so help me God'.

"Clement Osborne Payne, you are hereby charged with unlawful assembly, and refusing to obey the lawful order of an officer of His Majesty's constabulary. How do you plead?"

"Not guilty your worship."

Payne sits in the prisoner's dock. He shows no fear. He sits erect. His handsome face reflects a calm that infuriates his prosecutors and the prosecution. He is immaculately dressed in a suit with matching waistcoat and tie. His hair, parted to one side, is atop a slightly balding head and adds an air of elegance his detractors wish was not there, but it is.

The evidence is presented and the trial is short. The white judge, semi-resplendent in his wig and gown, intones the sentence.

"Mr. Payne, this court, having found you guilty of the

charges, imposes a fine of ten pounds in thirty days or thirty days in jail."

A murmur runs through the crowded courthouse, rolls outside, and is reflected from the masses gathered outside.

"Where he going to get ten pounds from?"

The brilliant, ambitious young lawyer rises to his feet.

"Your honor, I appear as *amicus curiae* on behalf of Mr. Payne and hereby begs leave to appeal against this unjust sentence."

Another murmur runs through the packed gallery. A man whispers to his neighbor:

"Boy that Grantley Adams is a smart lawyer. He going to go far."

Adams has come to the courthouse on a different matter. He sees the large crowd—seven or eight hundred men, drawn there because of the Payne trial, and sees an opportunity to be seized.

The appeal is successful, but Payne returns to golden Square night after night with the same message. He is soon re-arrested.

The voice of the presiding judge is doleful in the silent courtroom.

"Clement Osborne Payne, this court has found you guilty of willfully making a false statement as to your place of birth, to wit, claiming to be a Barbadian when in truth you are a native of Trinidad. Your defense that as far as you know you have lived all your life in Barbados and have considered yourself to be a Barbadian, and further that your mother told you that your were Barbadian, and that 'she would never lie to you' does not negate the fact that you were born in Trinidad. It is the judgment of this court that you be deported. There will be no bail, and you are to be taken henceforth to Glendairy Prison awaiting deportation."

The word spreads like the wind.

From Carrington's Village they come in large crowds. From

Suttle Street, Duke's Alley, Conch's Alley, Church Village, the Greenfields, Lightfoot Lane, Reid Street. From every stinking impoverished nook and cranny. Bay Street, Bank Hall, Howell's Cross Road, from everywhere.

The pierhead is black with men. Black men. They wait. The wind blows steadily, patiently. They wait quietly, patiently.

Payne is surreptitiously put in a row-boat at the Harbor Police pier, and taken to the waiting ship. Still they wait. The air is calm. The breeze has stopped blowing.

"Where he is? Why they don't bring him an put him on board the boat?"

The crowd grows restless.

"But wait," a voice exclaims; a new arrival. "You all still waiting on Payne? You don't know that they put him on the boat already? The boat sail away ever since."

"What that you say?" A gruff voice replies, approaching the new-comer aggressively.

"Man you can't hear? You deaf or what? I say that the police put Payne on the boat already."

"Looka, this ent no time to make joke. These is serious times." His voice rises to an angrier pitch. More people gather around until the man is completely surrounded and hemmed in.

"You like you ent got no hearings or understandings. I tell you I see the police van come up to the big gate at de Harbor Police station in Bay street just as I was passing, an' I see them take out Payne. I know it is he because I was down by the Court House when they had him on trial. And I was up by Government House too. I see when they take him out. He was handcuff with he hands behind he back. Then they hustle him out to the boat from the Harbor Police Jetty. The boat sailing already."

The wavelets breaking against the pier are ruffled and their sound can be heard in the stillness. The breeze picks up and grows in intensity. The waves get larger and smash themselves against the walls of the careenage.

"You all hear that?" The man's mood is ugly as he turns to the angry, disturbed, hungry men and women around him.

"YOU ALL HEAR THAT?" His voice is louder this time. "Because he open we eyes, they take him away. They take way the shepherd who is to lead we. Just cause he telling we how to put biscuits in we hungry bellies, they take he way. GOD BLIND DESE WHITE SONS O' BITCHES!"

The crowd mills around, anger in every flashing eye. They begin to walk toward Golden Square quickly, intently purposeful. Golden Square attracts them like a magnet.

The wind spreads the news quickly to every corner, every rum shop, and every bedroom. Payne gone! Their anger grows and soon the pent-up frustration of three hundred years explodes. Cars burning. Glass smashing. Stores looted. Sticks, stones, bottles, anything solid. A hurricane sweeping all before it.

The crowd sees the tight ranks of the police advancing toward it. They keep on. The police come closer. A stone. Another. A bottle and a coconut shell. Three, four, five stones, bottles and more coconut shells, and then the two forces meet and clash and lock. Sticks fall on baton and on head, clubs on shoulders and in stomachs. Fists batter, fingers gouge, hands clasp. Grunts, groans, harsh breathing. And they fight. Men fall, blood flows and drops on the hot tar. Black against Black. Brother against brother.

No whites. Why?

The police ranks break. They retreat. They run. The crowd pursues them with loud shouts. Down Broad Street, across Prince William Henry Street and Coleridge Street, through the gates of the Central Police station. The gates crash shut as bottles explode against them. And the wind howls.

The orgy of smashing continues. Street lamps broken, cars pushed into the sea. Anything upon which to vent their frustration. It goes on far into the night and the next day.

The wires whistle in the wind. They sing. The trees talk loudly with the wind. Stores broken. Everything broken except the spirit. They are uncontrollable in their fury.

The wind takes the message into the countryside. Unrest takes the whole island by storm. A chance to get food. Potato fields raided, pork barrels emptied, biscuits, corned beef. Food! Food! No more hunger.

The Riot Act is read.

Guns with bullets. Police and the Army.

"You hear what happen?"

"No tell me."

"Elvira son get kill with a shot that one of those policemen fire off."

Fourteen dead. Forty-seven wounded. Five hundred lock up. Order.

No breeze. Payne gone!

Daddy

The years between the riots and your father's death were short and flew by quickly. He was absent most of the time and your remembrances of him are of toys and glimpses of him weaving the multicolored cotton belts and zapatas* using the beadstead as a loom, and discipline. But you don't remember much of his appearance except that he was tall and handsome with slightly balding and receding hair.

"Didn't I tell you to be home by six?"

"Yes daddy."

"When I say to be home by six, it means you are to be in the house by six."

"But the Catholic bell was ringing just as I turn the corner and I run fast."

Whack! The blow falls across your tight bottom.

"When I say six, I mean six."

When the next blow falls the tears flow. Have they ever stopped?

"Where is daddy?"

"He got a job as a fireman on one of the Harrison Line boats."

His first job in three years, and he goes into the bowels of hell—a fireman on a steamship. Into the lowest depths of the ship. Black hold. Black coal. Black man.

You are already in your coffin, daddy.

Shovel the black coal into the hungry, flaming, maw with a black shovel. A never-ending process. No respite, no breath of air. Lungs bursting, chest heaving, muscles bulging. Black muscles in a Black body, in a black ship, on a black sea. After three years, stomach ulcers, or 'black lung'. Cigarettes, coal dust, hunger, worry. Three years without work.

Christ, daddy, how did you survive? Three years with a family, and nothing to restore your pride, your manhood. They say he waited too long to have the operation. Didn't they know they kept him too long without work? Didn't they care? Murderers! Are you there God? Did you know? Are You? God! God! GODDD! GODDD!

Black man in a black hole. Burning furnace, burning stomach. Death!

Daddy, where are you? I hardly know you. Where are you? I am only seven. See? Mum crying. Did you know you couldn't survive the trip? Where is your grave? Unmarked? Untended? Forgotten? Where is Bermuda? Away from your loved ones. Murdered! Three years. You were BLACK.

And then he was gone, forever.

Your mother took over insisting on attention to education and scouting and discipline and activities to keep you on the straight and narrow until your secondary school was over.

Your remembrances of that time, a time when life was simple, when the village and the people and the country were as one, existing and surviving by helping and comforting each other; sharing joys and sorrows and war and Ta-la-la-la, and Ga-Ga who couldn't escape the stultifying restrictions of a poverty -stricken society. In another time and another place their fates might have been different, but now they were victims.

War

It is five o'clock in the afternoon. You know it is five o'clock because Ta-la-la-la is 'bringing over the news'. He is a short, stocky, bow-legged man with 'goadies'—enlarged testicles—who has easily the loudest voice anywhere on the island. He has honed it to a pitch where it could be heard over a hundred yards away without any artificial amplification. Everybody likes to hear his version of 'the news' which he would 'bring over' with the incentive of a few pennies.

Today the patrons are anxious to hear his version of a stabbing incident in Payne's Bay, and the international news about the war. Ta-la-la-la always gives the international news first, introducing it with the Greenwich time signal, and his own introductory musical interlude:

«Ta-la-la la la la la la la,
Ta lalalalalalala,
Archie Bryner, lalalalalalala,
Cum ber rum ber rum,
Archie Bryner,
Cum ber rum ber rum, Archie Bryner,
Cum ber rum, ber rum Archie Bryner,
Ta-la-la-la-la-la-la-la-la bim bam.»

Nobody knows what the words mean, but the tune is melodious.

"Today, British warplanes drop five hundred thousand million bombs pun Berlin. Germans was running everywhere. Nuhbody ent see Hitler. Mr. Churchill say England expect every man to do his duty; he ent say nothing 'bout women though.

HERE GOES OUR LOCAL NEWS!

A man an' a woman... I say a man an' a wo-man,
Down Payne's Bay... Down Paynes Bay,
Fighting a ten roun' bout... fighting a ten roun' bout
Bing bang.... fight start.
De man move in... de woman move out,
De man swing in... de woman duck out.
De man wibble an wobble.... de woman wobble
an wibble.
De man hit de woman wid a right cross long
side she head,
De woman fall down.
De man pick she up an leggo a leff...
De woman slip way
De woman pick up a big able twelve inch knife
and DRIVE it in de man chess bone.
De man fall down. Blood spurting like a hose.
Bing Bang! Fight done! Man dead!"

The crowd which has gathered in the bus stand out by the Empire Theatre to hear 'the news' almost collapses with laughter at this account of the stabbing incident, and wait for him to 'sign off' with his 'signature tune' and 'gun salute'.

"Whoop! ...Pee Dow!
Whoop!!...PEEE Dow!
WHOOOP...PEEEE Dow!!!"

Before he could finish, however, the sound descends on the country. The loud boom coming from the direction of the harbor coincides with the ground-shaking rumble which fills the air. The plate glass windows in front of Cole's garage, near the Empire theatre, come crashing to the ground, smashing into a thousand pieces or more, followed by those at Eckstein's garage across the street. There is silence. Everything and everyone is silent. It is a questioning silence. It is a silence of anticipation, a silence of wonder, a silence of fear.

And then it comes. Another crashing boom with a sound and rumble like the thunder of a rain-laden, cloud-black thunder storm, and with the sound comes the realization of what is happening.

"The Cornwallis get torpedo!" Somebody shouts.

And then the sirens start wailing and all the Black people run to the beaches and waterfront around Carlisle Bay to see what is going on. And all the white people in Hastings and Maxwell head for the hills and Bathsheba, on the other side of the island.

The war has finally come to Barbados directly. From the beginning of the war you are aware that it is happening somewhere else, although you see the warships in their gray paint coming and going. Your best friend's father is a sailor on one of the Coast Guard vessels which have come up from Trinidad, and you get to go on board sometimes. One of the Harbor Police launches is converted into a submarine chaser, although it is not very fast, even after the conversion. But you like to watch the American Torpedo boats. Now those are fast, as they race up and down the bay, the bows rise in the air, and the water sprays on either side, and they sit on their backsides in the water and move. They are like the thoroughbred race horses which run on the Garrison. They never seem to be still, and always seem to want to take off at any moment in any direction. They patrol inside and outside the submarine nets which are made of heavy steel mesh, and stretch to the bottom of the sea along the entire length of Carlisle Bay. Ships can only get inside through a gate near the end of the net near the

Aquatic Club, and which is opened by a small tug boat.

You sit on the Harbor Police jetty or on Brown's beach and watch the hustle and bustle and play at submarines and 'mine-laying' in the water with your friends. To make a mine you get a cork and stick pins all around to represent the detonators, attach it to a piece of string and a stone, and throw it as far as you can into the sea. It is fun to try and find the mine, especially when four or five of you, innocent and ignorant, dive together into the water with lots of splashing, each trying to find it first. And it would be there on the white sand far beneath the surface of the clear, emerald-green water, waiting with its silver detonators. Waiting, just like the other mines of life, just waiting. But you are innocent now, and only know of these mines later when the detonators cause more damage—inside.

War is ration certificates and lining up for hours in Collymore Rock—where the Convent is now located—to get food. Everything is in short supply, but some ships still come to bring food, and stay within the confines of the submarine net for protection. Sometimes the Sergeant Major at the Harbor Police station and his children go out in a row boat to look at ships which have been torpedoed, but which managed to limp into port. You wonder about the men who work on those ships, who die on them, who survive on them, and who live past the torpedoes, the sinkings, and the sea and hot sun. They are brave men.

Many of you have fathers who work on them, and you feel proud because your father is one of them. Many of you have fathers who die on them 'in the service of the King'. Many inhabitants of Little England* are proud to die 'in the service of the King'. Your father dies while 'in the service of the King', but your mother can't get any compensation because he was not torpedoed; he died in hospital. Had he died after being torpedoed, he would have died 'in the service of the King'.

The Cornwallis is a cargo vessel. No one knows how the

German submarine has been able to breach the submarine net, but one thing is sure, the Cornwallis has been torpedoed, and the whole area becomes a hive of activity right away. The torpedo boats come roaring out of the careenage like wild dogs, and the converted Harbor Police launch comes rushing out also, far behind, but trying to give the impression that it is just as ferocious. They go rushing all over the bay, going everywhere and nowhere in particular. The people say "they frighten to go outside the net", that "the submarine long gone by the time they get started" and that "it is a waste of time", and "what they going do anyhow, even if they meet up with the submarine?" This causes great hilarity on the beach. Bajans laugh at everything, and find a joke in even the most serious situations.

Then the laughter stops abruptly. Another torpedo crashes into the Cornwallis. The noise of the explosion and the geyser of oil and water and steam erupting into the air from the stricken ship silences everyone. Great activity is seen on the ship as it begins to sink, but then it rights itself as the pumps begin to function. Then Carlisle bay becomes alive again with boats and people rushing to and fro.

The Cornwallis has a big hole in its side, and there is oil on the water all over the bay.

And then things start to appear in the night. Condensed milk in oil-covered tins, and oil-covered cheese, and oil-covered thread, and all sorts of oil-covered food and clothes, sometimes even a single oil-covered shoe. The Cornwallis is on her way to England, full of food.

Bajan men, especially those from around Brown's Beach or Burke's Beach, are good swimmers and divers. A lot of them grew up diving for pennies thrown overboard by sailors and passengers on ships. Some of them can dive from one side of a boat under the bottom and come up the other side. The divers bring their booty back to shore even though they are forbidden to go near the wounded ship. They go at night without lights, and dive up what has spilled out of the holds through the hole beneath the waterline, and these things circulate.

God gives Bajans some of that food which was going to England. A lot of people say "God know what we going through, an' that is why the German submarine able to torpedo the boat", "Bajans is God own children". And nobody could convince them otherwise. And then Mr. Taylor gets the salvage rights, and brings the balance of the cargo from the damaged hold to sell. Cloth and thread and shoes and sardines and cheese and curdled condensed milk, and all sorts of other things, all smelly, all oil-covered, but to be sold.

He makes lots of money. He is white. He owns a clothing store in Swan Street, a hotel in Hastings and a funeral establishment. He is often heard to comment:

"I clothe them, I house them, I feed them and I bury them."

Mr. Taylor is very rich.

Innocence

You are seventeen when you meet the whore in the bus stand. She is young, probably not more than sixteen, but she looks like she might be thirty. Her breasts are pointed, she has no brassieres. Her hair is plaited, but seems not to have been washed for some time. The dress, threadbare in some places, shows a dark stain under the armpits, visible in the yellow glow of the street lamp. Not bad-looking though, with eyes dark and expressive, lips well-shaped although the downturn at the corners hint at bitterness. Nostrils flared over hollow cheeks with dimples and high cheek bones even though the dimples are masked by the thinness of her jaws. Her hips are broad for her height, and her legs are well-shaped. She has not bothered to put on her shoes properly and they drag tiredly on her dirty feet. She could be a beauty under different circumstances.

"How much you charging?" you ask hesitantly.

Her eyes shine in anticipation, not at the prospect of sex, but at the thought of the money. She has lost the ability to enjoy sex long ago. Is she yet eighteen?

"Five dollars." Her voice is soft, with the hint of an accent.

"That's too much."

"How much you got?"

"Only sixty cents."

"Well we can't go in the hotel and get a room for that. I guess we could go in the yard and do it standing up."

"All right."

The bargain is struck. Your knees are shaking. You follow behind as she goes through the narrow alley leading off from

Bay Street. Your shoes slip on banana skins as you walk. She pushes the galvanize gate which scrapes against the ground with a harsh ripping sound as she lets you in ahead of her.

It is dark, but you can make out the shapes of the contents of the yard by the faint glow of a kerosene lamp which shines through a crack in the house. She pushes her way between the mango crates—shipped from St. Lucia with their black speckled loads—into a corner, then stops, turns, and holds out her hand for the money. You can't see her face.

"Gimme the money!"

You hand her the sixty cents. The scream breaks upon your ears, with a sound like the cacophony of a thousand cymbals. It comes again. Light floods the yard as the door of the house bursts open. You now see that men have been playing dominoes inside, all this observed in one split second, as the adrenaline forces your legs into action even before your brain comprehends the reason.

You run! Fast! You smash into the teetering galvanize gate, hearing its clatter as it falls, hearing the laughter of the men and the shrill cackle of the whore. Shame floods you. Is there no honesty? You are so innocent. Born in innocence, baser instincts gaining the ascendancy, in a hole, a pit, a prison. Whore. Thief. Pimp. Murderer. Poverty. Dirt. Disease. Rotten mangoes. Rotten oranges. Rotten people. SHIT! Nelson Street! Are you there God?

For the rest of your life you never think of patronizing a whore. You are cured of that desire. But your proximity to Nelson Street and your passages through that area help guide you on your own passage through your youth, showing you all aspects of life and personal interactions. They teach you lessons about life, love and hate, cruelty and hurt, and survival. You remember now. You remember the story of Ga-Ga's love for Frankie and the tragic end to his life from which there was no escape, a life of conflicting personalities trapped within the same body, which ended in death.

Ga-Ga

Ga-Ga was a buller*. He was what Eunice called a 'fish-and-float buller'. He was a cheap whore. He lived in Jordan's Lane and had come over from St. Lucia a couple of years earlier. He and Frankie lived together, and since Frankie had become his steady man, Ga-Ga had been faithful. He even thought about talking to Frankie about getting married.

Before he met Frankie, life had been a constant round of men: young men, old men, all sizes and colors. It was surprising how many 'respectable' men had sex with Ga-Ga, even white men and tourists. Sometimes he would really dress up. Like the time when he entered the beauty contest and went to the hotels in Hastings. He would just stand up outside the Accra or the Royal to be picked up, or sometimes the taxi men would bring the tourists to him, right down in Suttle Street at the corner of Conch's Alley. Most of these men wanted straight sex, but sometimes they wanted other things. Ga-Ga did those other things.

One night, at a dance in the Park, three men got him drunk and then they all had sex with him behind the Spartan Pavilion, near the public toilets. When they finished he was too sore to even sit down. A week later he found out that he had the clap*.

After the course of penicillin at the Health Centre had cured him, he moved from Suttle Street to Reid Street, and then a few weeks later to Jordan's lane, one of the alleys leading off from Nelson Street. That was when he met Frankie. He was standing by the bus stand railings one evening talking with some other 'bullers' who used to lime* there looking for pickups and making remarks about the people who were passing by. A fight suddenly broke out between Boysie, who was Courtney's man, and Valerie, who wanted to live with Courtney. Nobody knew what started the fight, but since Ga-Ga was Valerie's friend and Valerie was receiving several blows from Boysie, Ga-Ga jumped in. He gave Boysie a slap in his face while Valerie held on to Boysie's shirt and ripped it off. Boysie caught hold of Ga-Ga's hair, pulled out all the curlers, and delivered a bite to his face that almost ripped out the piece of flesh. Ga-Ga backed off and then sprang onto Boysie again.

All this time Valerie was scratching Boysie all over his face and neck and slapping him, at the same time swearing and saying what he was going to do to him. Suddenly Boysie delivered a back-kick that caught Valerie in his testicles, causing him to double up in pain, hollering and crying. He retired from the fight. He held on to his testicles with big tears running down his face, and shouting remarks about what he was going to do to Boysie when he recovered.

While all this was happening a big crowd gathered around the fighters. Quicker than the wind spreading a cane fire, the news quickly spread across the Bridge, down Marhill Street, and through Swan Street and Baxter's Road.

"The bullers fighting in de bus stan'!"

Everybody ran to see the fight, wanting to get there before it was finished.

By this time Boysie had ripped off Ga-Ga clothes exposing his panties, and blood was all over the place.

A woman shouted: "Somebody part dem nuh, wunna gwine leh dem kill one annuder?"

"Looka woman, shut your mouth. You know nobody can't get in bullers fights, cause then all of them does hold on pun you and beat you up," a man with a bearded face answered.

"But I didn't know they does wear panties," another voice exclaimed.

"After all, them is women too ent it?"

Everybody burst out laughing. Meanwhile Boysie and Ga-Ga were still fighting.

"Looka how de two a' them scratching and pulling out one another hair."

"But who start this scandal?"

"I ent know, but you can bet it is over another man."

"Somebody call the Police!"

"Part them nuh! Part them!"

"No, let them fight. I never see bullers fight before."

Ga-Ga and Boysie were lashing out, swearing and crying, all at the same time. Their clothes were torn off and both had been badly scratched. Valerie was still holding onto his testicles as if he had in fact been castrated, and was passing all sorts of nasty remarks at Boysie.

That is when Frankie got involved.

Frankie was a lighter man* who worked on the wharf pulling the eight-foot oars on the lighters which transported cargo between ships anchored in Carlisle Bay and the wharf. He was big, strong, and good-looking, and he wasn't afraid of anybody. He liked women and men, and was well-known among the bullers. He knew all of them, and did not care who saw him mixing with them even though he knew how the people in his community felt about them.

Decent people didn't have anything to do with bullers, but he wasn't embarrassed to be with them. He liked Ga-Ga and had danced with him a few times at the Liberty dance hall, holding him tight and letting him feel his erection. Ga-Ga liked that and drew Frankie closer.

Nobody knew where he came from or why he got into the fight. It was like he dropped out of the sky. He just appeared between the two fighters. He gave Boysie a punch alongside his head that knocked him down to the ground. Then he grabbed Ga-Ga, twisting his hand behind his back, judo-style, and pushed him up against the railings next to the road. Ga-

Ga was swearing in his high-pitched voice that he wanted to get back in the fight so that he could "tear out Boysie guts". Frankie gave him a 'spring butt' that knocked all the sense out him, and he didn't want to fight any more.

Frankie took over the situation.

"Valerie, you an' Boysie get home quick, before I kick in both of wunna ass!"

"But who you think you is tekking up Ga-Ga fire-rage?" Boysie answered in his falsetto voice, still dizzy from the punch that Frankie delivered to his head, but pretending to be bold.

"If you don't get out of here real fast, I going beat your ass hole to a frazzle. You want to end up in the hospital? Why the hell you all got to cause this confusion?" Frankie's voice was almost a whisper, but everyone heard it in the silence. It had venom.

The crowd was so big now that the cars and buses blocked the road. People were leaning out of car windows to get a look at the commotion. All the St. Lucians from Jordan's Lane and Jessamy Alley came down to see who was fighting with Ga-Ga, and no traffic was moving in Fairchild street.

It was only then that the policeman turned up. He was one of the Harbor Policemen from the Bridge Post on Bay Street who dressed up like one of the sailors on Lord Nelson's ship. He was soft-spoken and easy-going, although everybody knew that he was very strong because he was a body-building champion. He was a serious policeman who was not to be underestimated. He told the crowd to disperse, and they started to move along, although quite slowly. He was going to carry Ga-Ga, Boysie and Valerie to the station and charge them for creating a disturbance, but when Frankie told him that everything was under control and that he was going take Ga-Ga home, he said "alright", and told everyone to go about their business. So everybody started to move more quickly, the entire time talking about the fight, and bullers, and everything else in that connection.

One of the vendors, sitting with her tray of sugar cakes, comforts* and nuts near the entrance to Nelson Street, remarked to one of her neighboring vendors:

"Ivy, you know dat ef Ta-la-la-la didn't in de alms house he would have to 'broadcast' dis scandal pun he local news."

"You right girl," Ivy answered, "I can just hear he now: *Here goes our local news, a man an' a woman,* no leh me change dat, *a buller an' a woman.*"

"No you can't say it dat way, he woulda say *two women had a fight in de bus stan, over a man.*"

They had a hearty laugh over the incident.

Ivy became very thoughtful. "But I din' know Ta-la-la-la was in de alms house. I miss he an' was wondering what become of he."

"Well you know how it is," was the answer, "ef yuh poor an yuh ent got nutting to look forward to nor nobody to look after you dat is where yuh does en up. He wasn't no idiot, he even used to preach sometimes, but he couldn't go to seccondary school, an de few pennies he get from 'broadcasting' the news wasn't enough to keep he, an dat is where he en' up. I hear he getting down and going soon pass away."

"Dat is life." Ivy sighed as she served a customer with a pack of nuts.

Traffic was soon flowing smoothly again. Frankie and Ga-Ga went across the alley after Frankie got a piece of cotton with some iodine and a piece of elastoplast dressing from Clarke's Drug store. A big crowd followed both of them all the way through the alley, all the time laughing and pointing, until they got to Ga-Ga's house.

That was one thing about Bajans. A big crowd gathered at anything that happened. They would collect at every 'bum knock an' spree'*, but if two drops of rain started to fall everyone scattered as though the devil in hell was after them.

Since Frankie 'spring-butt' him, Ga-Ga's head hurt really badly and he was crying all the time. It was only when they reached home and Frankie fixed up his wounds, gave him two aspirins and lay in bed with him, that he stopped crying. He soon dropped off to sleep with his arms around Frankie, and his legs between Frankie's.

Even though Frankie was big and tough and had a reputation as a hard man on the outside, he seemed to have a soft spot for Ga-Ga. Maybe he realized that Ga-Ga needed the protection he could give him at this time in his life, and needed him. Ga-Ga was not a big person, he was what people called 'high brown', with a small face, a petite body, and was not very strong. He walked with mincing steps and spoke with a soft, affected accent. Maybe that is what attracted Frankie. Whatever it was, he seemed to be genuinely attracted to Ga-Ga.

Ga-Ga awoke early and had breakfast ready when Frankie got up. They ate together and when Ga-Ga offered to cook for Frankie every day, he accepted the offer.

Since Frankie became his man only one thing was wrong, and Ga-Ga felt bad about it. Frankie not only loved to have sex with him, but he used to sneak off every now and then to have sex with Eunice, who lived in a little two-room hut behind the bakery in Nelson Street. Ga-Ga didn't like the idea of Eunice making love to his man, because every time he met up with Eunice when he went to the market in Fairchild Street to buy his meat and vegetables, she always passed some nasty remark. He really wanted to confront her, but he knew that Frankie would get angry, so he held his peace every time.

Eunice was young, in her early twenties, short, with a good shape although her backside was 'cocked off like a sparrow bird'. She was nice-looking with thick lips and two large breasts that looked like young grapefruits sticking out of her dress, always threatening to fall out. She never wore brassieres.

She always had a twinkle in her eye, and seemed to find something to laugh at all the time. She had a stall in the market which she used to display her tray with oranges, limes and sometimes mangoes to sell. She didn't have any money in the bank because, as she always said: "it ent no sense having money in de bank, an' yuh stomach asking yuh backbone questions". She had only attended elementary school, but since her mother put her out of the house after catching her daughter in bed with her boyfriend, she decided to be independent and move away from home completely. She felt that she was old enough to live alone and wanted to be free, without the restrictions her mother tried to impose on her movements and actions.

Eunice was an enigma. She was bright enough to enter secondary school, but was seemingly possessed of an 'own-way' streak of stubbornness that resisted all authority. She seemed destined to be bad, and even though her mother tried her best to keep her along a decent path, she chose her own path. She was not a law-breaker—she had an aversion to dishonesty—but she did what she pleased and was not prepared to back down from anyone. She was a free spirit who thrived in the atmosphere of Nelson Street. The day she left home she rented a room over the bakery in Nelson Street and decided to 'set herself in business', as she said. She got a tray built by one of the joiners working in the alley and started her career by begging a man for some mangoes from his tree and selling them in the market, even though she didn't have a license. She soon remedied that. One night, she seduced the market superintendent inside one of the market stalls, and the next day she had the license.

Eunice knew how to take care of herself. Two things in life interested her: eating and having sex. If she could get it, she would have sex every night and day.

Most of the time when she met up with him, Ga-Ga just gave her a cut-eye* and passed on, tossing his head in the air and wiggling his small behind. This always made Eunice burst out laughing. She would laugh so much that tears would roll down her cheeks and drop on her big breasts which would be shaking like two breadfruits on a tree in a high wind. Ga-Ga tried to ignore it, but it used to hurt him inside, and every time he got back home he would sit and cry out of frustration. He wanted to be somebody, but he didn't know how to be somebody. He was what he was. Nothing could change that. Frankie was all he had.

He begged Frankie to leave Eunice, but every time he brought up the subject it would end in a quarrel, and most of the time Frankie finished off the argument by beating him. He took Frankie's lashes without fighting back because he knew he could never win. He knew how strong Frankie was and he knew he could get hurt badly. He couldn't understand Frankie's personality though. One moment he could be kind and loving, considerate and generous, and the next minute he could become cruel and even vicious. Whenever Ga-Ga tried to probe into his background, he closed up and changed the subject. After a time he gave up trying. He never found out who Frankie truly was.

Frankie was late for dinner. Ga-Ga had finished cooking and was keeping the food warm in the enamel bowl on the two-burner kerosene oil stove. After the last quarrel with Frankie two days before which ended with him getting beaten badly, he was especially quiet around the house. He did everything to please his man. He went out of his way to cook his favorite meals. Frankie liked breadfruit cou-cou* with stewed liver. That day Ga-Ga had gone all the way down to the Cheapside market to get a piece of liver from a butcher who used to be his boyfriend. He knew that he would get a good piece of meat from him. He chose the breadfruit carefully, even going to the extent of berating one hawker who told him he was "feeling up de breadfruit too much".

He wasn't going to let anybody or anything stop him from giving Frankie the best dinner that he knew how to make. He sang as he went about his work in the kitchen. He was happy. Frankie was his man and he loved him. Frankie gave him money to pay the rent and buy groceries, and occasionally he gave him some to spend on himself. What he liked best though, was the way Frankie made love to him. Whenever that happened, he felt protected and secure when he fell asleep in Frankie's arms. This was what he never got from any of his other lovers, or even his mother.

Frankie had not made love to him for almost a week now, and Ga-Ga wanted him really badly. Even as he peeled the breadfruit in the kitchen with the afternoon sunlight coming in through the broken jalousies* of the broken windows, he started to get an erection. Thinking about how good Frankie was when they fondled each other, he put down the half-peeled breadfruit, went into the bedroom, and masturbated. With a loud sigh, almost a sob, Ga-Ga had his moment of ecstasy and ejaculated.

He bent and pulled up the panties and skin-fitting pants. He wondered whether he should change his panties and put on the blue nylon ones—the ones with the flowers on the front, but decided against it. He always chose his panties carefully when he went shopping in the stores on Broad Street. He gave the store clerks a hard time, frustrating them with the time he took to choose his garments. He felt that 'women' should take their time making their choices, and after all, he felt like a woman. Time had passed quicker than he realized and now he would have to hurry to get the dinner finished before Frankie came home.

The meal finished, he started to sew a pair of skin-tight tangerine slacks that he wanted to wear to a moonlight excursion. He sewed by the light of the kerosene lamp at the dining room table, and was almost finished when he heard the eleven o'clock news on the Rediffusion radio hanging in the corner of the room.

"Where Frankie is?" He wondered aloud. He had bathed and powdered with the sweetest-smelling powder he could find in Clarke's Drug Store, and he had even run the ironing comb through his hair and put in a few curls. He wanted Frankie to be pleased when he came home. Knowing that Frankie didn't like to kiss him when he had bristles on his face, he had condescended to shave. This was one of the most distasteful things Ga-Ga had to do, for he loathed this constant reminder that he was not what he thought he was, and wanted to be. He hated this constant reminder of what he really was.

After his bath he had put on a new panty and a pair of purple slacks which fitted tightly, and showed the imprint of his panties. The silk polka-dot shirt was knotted just above his navel so that the skin showed between the bottom of his shirt and the top of the slacks. He wanted Frankie.

"Where is he this time of the night?" he asked loudly to himself.

He put down the sewing, went to the window, and looked up and down the alley. The stomach-sickening smell which lingered in the air constantly did not permeate his brain. He was immune to squalor. It didn't exist for him. His eyes saw the ragged woman reach into the barrel of rotten mangoes waiting for the stuff cart* to pick them up, and pick out two of them. He saw her scoop out the rotten portions of the fruit with her thumb, peel off the black speckled skin, and greedily stuff the yellow portion of the flesh into her mouth, the juice running in a fetid stream down the two sides of her mouth. It didn't register as anything unusual.

He went back inside and began to sew again. He was becoming worried. "Frankie tekking too long to get home!"

There was a knock on the door. He knew it wasn't Frankie, he never knocked. He went to the window and, looking out, saw one of his old friends, Timmie, who used to live in Eagle Hall with Blair.

"Timmie, is a long time since I ain't see you. What you doing out here this time of the night?"

"I come to get you. You don't know Frankie in hospital?"

Ga-Ga immediately started to feel faint. He put his hand on his heart, and a tightness came to his throat.

"Lord have mercy, no! Yuh telling lies Timmie!"

"Is true! He and Eunice get in a fight near Gwen shop in Nelson Street, and she cut him up. He in the casualty now."

"OH GOD!" Ga-Ga bawled out loudly in anguish, holding his belly and bending down. "I beg Frankie every since not to have nothing to do with that wutless whore Eunice, and all I beg and beg, he won't hear to me, and look what happen now."

"Well you better come to the casualty now and see how he look."

Ga-Ga hastily put on a pair of slippers, and without locking the door, ran down the alley with Timmie behind him. At the corner he almost slipped on a overturned garbage can which was blocking the gutter and causing the dirty water to flow across the street from one side to the other.

Nelson Street was jammed with donkey carts, bicycles, cars, and people. Gwen's shop, as usual, was overflowing with the crowd from the Plaza theatre, mostly the pit* crowd, smelly, dirty, sweaty, and rough. They were getting their midnight meals: pork cutters, sweet bread, cheese cutters and drinks. It was noisy and everybody was calling at the same time:

"Gimme a Gwen special an' a Martineau drink!"

"Every since I here calling for a quarter pound of cheese an' eight cents in biscuits. My money ent good or what?"

"Look, try and wait yuh turn like everybody else. You is a Rusheon?"

There was good-natured banter, with expletives here and there. These were familiar sights and sounds which Ga-Ga passed without noticing. Timmie was having a hard time keeping up with him as he turned into Wellington Street, and was almost running by the time they reached Jemmott's lane.

The casualty was full of people, and everybody was talking at the same time. It was really loud in there. Frankie was sitting on a chair with blood-stained bandages tied around his head and chest. His shirt was torn and bloody, and tied around his waist. His head, bowed and supported on his hands which were cupped underneath his chin, was moving from side to side.

"Oh God! Frankie, wha happen?" Ga-Ga shouted as he came through the door. "Wha happen to my man?" Tears sprang to his eyes when he caught sight of Frankie. Everybody in the casualty stopped talking at the same time and looked at Ga-Ga, then they turned and looked at Frankie. Frankie looked up and then held down his head. Ga-Ga came up to him with tears running down his face.

"Frankie, Frankie, you hurt bad?

"Oh shite!" Frankie exclaimed loudly so that everybody could hear. "Why the hell you din' stan' home?"

Stunned, Ga-Ga stopped.

"Timmie come and tell me how you get cut up, and I had to come and see what happen," he said. His eyes were appealing to Frankie for understanding.

"Well, you see. Now you can just haul your ass back out of here and leave me alone. I don't want you 'round here!"

"But let me help you, nuh. I just want to hold your hand or something. I would do anything to help. You know I love you real bad."

At this point everybody started murmuring and talking to each other and they could see that Frankie was very embarrassed, maybe for the first time in his life.

"Get to fuck out of here. I don't want you 'round me. And to besides, when I get fix up here I going home at Eunice, so don't bother me no more. We finish! I done with you!"

Each word was like a stab-wound to Ga-Ga's heart. Ga-Ga couldn't believe his ears. Frankie was leaving him to live with Eunice? After what she had done to him? His Frankie that he loved so much? His man was leaving him? Above all, going to live with a woman?

His head was spinning as he ran out of the casualty. Some of the people laughed out loud, and the sound of it seemed to follow him even when he was out of range. He stopped running and started to walk as though he was in a daze. He felt like he was going mad. It was the laughter, again.

No more Frankie? How was he going to live without Frankie? And to lose him to a woman? A woman like Eunice?

He heard every laugh from her and it seemed like his head was bursting. He had to do something. He was going to do something. He didn't know when he reached the kitchen. He didn't know when he left the house or when he reached the gap by the bakery. He didn't know when he called out to Eunice, or when he started to curse her in a voice whose falsetto was made higher by his anger and hurt.

"Eunice! Eunice! You isn't anything but a worthless whore, who only want to take away other women men. All like you ent deserve no having from decent men like Frankie. Why de hell you don't keep way from my man?"

"You can kiss my ass!" Eunice shouted as she came flying out the door and faced up to Ga-Ga. This time she wasn't joking. Her face was contorted with anger and she was ready to fight.

"My body clean, and that is why Frankie like it. See? It clean!" And with that she lifted up her dress and exposed herself. She didn't have on any panties. "I catch your man with it and I going keep he with it. He done pushing he cock up in you. I got he and I going keep he. You hear! I going keep he. And you can kiss my ass, again!!!"

Their faces were almost touching.

"YOU CAN'T KEEP FRANKIE, CAUSE IF I CAN'T HAVE HE, NEEDER ONE UH WE ENT GOING KEEP HE!"

Ga-Ga's voice was almost a scream in its intensity. There was no conscious effort in the act; just a flash of light on steel, a grunt, a widening of the eyes, and Eunice's hands tried to stem the flood of red liquid as her intestines spilled between her fingers. Ga-Ga turned away and, walking slowly, passed through the silenced crowd which had gathered around the combatants. They moved aside. Eunice sagged to the ground. Ga-Ga turned the corner and was walking down Nelson Street toward the careenage before the first remark was made.

"She dead?"

"She got to be, look how she belly hanging out!"

"Somebody send for the ambulance!"

"Call the 999!"

"Ga-Ga gone mad!"

"Somebody go and hold he. Don't let he escape!"

"No soul, you see de big knife he got in he hand?"

"Well somebody got to do something for Eunice. But what to do?"

All this time Eunice's belly was hanging loosely and moving slowly like a snake on the ground, and she was not making a sound. Only her eyes were wide open, her gut was in her hands, and her mouth was moving as though she wanted to say something, but no sound was coming out.

Ga-Ga was still walking with his eyes wide open, but he wasn't seeing anything, only the tears running down his face and dropping to the ground and mixing with the blood from the knife he was still holding in his hand, drop by drop, like the semen from his penis.

He almost reached the careenage before the people realized where he was, and then they started running and shouting out his name. Then he was walking a little faster, and the tears were running faster, and he was breathing faster. But his eyes were still wide open, all this time without a sound coming from his throat even though his mouth wide open.

He saw his childhood. He saw his mother forcing him to sew clothes, and giving him dolls, and making him wash clothes and cook the food. He saw her plaiting and curling his hair even though he was old enough to have it cut like all the other boys, and he saw her dressing him in girls' clothes, and not letting him play with the other boys.

He heard the laughter—always the laughter. He hated his mother. She wanted a girl. She made him a girl. He wanted to be a man, but he didn't know how to be one. He wanted to be

47

different, but he never learned how.

The water, dark and warm, soothed and comforted him. It cradled him as he sank back into the womb. No more laughter. No more tears. No more love. No more Frankie. No feelings. No feelings. No more. Death embraced him in her arms and cradled him in her bosom.

You heard about the tragedy on the news, not broadcast by Ta-la-la-la, but on the Rediffusion radio. Ga-Ga's body turned up floating in the careenage two days after. The bloated body was taken to the funeral home, the same funeral home that housed Eunice's body. Frankie made arrangements to have both Ga-Ga and Eunice buried together. He broke down as the two bodies were lowered into the graves. He was never the same after that. For days he just sat at the window to Ga-Ga's house staring into the distance. He became a shadow of his former self.

Then he disappeared. It was rumored that he got a job on a Lady Boat* and went to Halifax. Some say he got a job on the Cornwallis when she resumed sailing, but went down with her when she was again torpedoed by another German submarine and sank with all hands.

For months afterward the story of Ga-Ga and Frankie was the talk of the town.

Security

You graduate from Combermere. Combermere Secondary school is not as costly as Harrison College, but it is where your vestry scholarship has taken you. It is the school that you grow to love. It is the school that teaches you the lessons of life and survival with the best. It gives you the foundation. It supplies the civil servants, of which you are one working in 'the service' for six years before you think about going to university.

As a people we have been brought up to believe that the civil service is the pinnacle. When one works in the civil service that is something. One has achieved. You are somebody. The salary is small but 'security' is more important than the accumulation of wealth, so we are told. We will never be able to earn enough to make ourselves independent. We will have to work all our lives to be able to keep up the payments on a house mortgage—if we could get one—but 'security' is ours.

The Civil Service is for Black people. Meanwhile the white people, some of whom do not even complete secondary school, get their jobs at Musson, and DaCosta, and Mannings and all the other white-owned stores, commercial companies, and 'The Bank'*.

Of course they don't get jobs as porters or messengers although their levels of education deserve no higher. They begin as cash boys, cashiers or office clerks, and within a short time get prominent positions in the firms, along with commensurate salaries supplemented by annual bonuses and the opportunity to rise higher in the company.

Back in the post office or audit department and other government offices, or in the police force, the Blacks have 'security'.

No white people work in the civil service apart from some englishmen from the colonial office. When the white english operators at Cable and Wireless leave to go back to their homes in the 'mother country', new operators are hired. But they are not Black. They are 'high-brown', a subtle change, but not a real change. They are paid more than the Civil Servants, but they don't have 'security'.

"Don't mind those fellows up there. They could get chase away any time," you are told by older and presumably wiser heads when you point out the differences in income. "Those fellows almost all work for over twenty years at Cable and Wireless. They don't have security." But they are better off.

It has taken you over a year to get a job as a temporary clerk in the service. Before that you work as an apprentice electrician. You have your School Certificate, with good results after your five years of secondary school, which makes you eligible for a job in the service and 'security'. You just cannot get it though. Jobs are hard to find. Few are available.

Needless to say, your education and School Certificate are of no use when you go to the white-owned places in response to advertisements. There are always no vacancies, although the position would be advertised again.

Some of your friends get jobs as cabin boys on the Lady Boats—Canadian freighters which travel between The Maritimes and the West Indies—and put to sea. Your mother still works as a maid at the white ladies' club, the Ladies Lyceum Club in Bolton's Lane.

Why are you taught to place such emphasis on 'security'? Is it the indoctrination of the rulers? Those of the 'stiff upper lip' from whom we inherit the system, the mores, the manners, the culture, the afternoon tea, and cricket?

You finally get taken on as an apprentice electrician. As an apprentice you get to work at six o'clock every morning. You get up at five and ride the three miles to the workshop before you and the other workers head off to the job at the sugar factories or homes or wherever the job is to be done. The work initially is difficult. It is always dirty, and sometimes frustrating. You learn to run wires and repair lights in the roofs of the factories, working in dirt inches thick on the rafters among rat droppings, not even conscious of the danger to your health. You sometimes work in the roofs of houses which are hot and airless, and at other times in cellars which are equally hot and airless. But you learn. For the first three weeks you don't get paid any money.

"You now learning. You can't expect to get any money," the foreman says.

Then you get sixty cents a week. You have a School Certificate. You are learning. Soon you can supplement that sixty cents by wiring a few houses and repairing a few electric irons. The island is progressing.

After a year of this you get a letter from the government. You are invited to sit the qualifying examination for entry into the civil service. You pass. You are on your way to 'security', from eleven shillings a week to forty dollars a month. You have a big jump in salary—a job as a temporary clerk, although 'security' is still two years away after the probationary period as a long grade clerk. After five years you finally achieve. You have reached the zenith and you have 'security'.

Your friend comes back from Columbia University with his degree. He is among the fortunate ones. Through him you learn that there are scholarships offered by universities all over the world. Study Abroad, the book which opens the door.

You apply and get a scholarship—a tuition waiver—you will have to find all other living expenses. You have no money. You only have 'security'.

You apply for study leave. It is rejected. The regulations don't provide for study leave outside of something immediately connected with your job. These are the colonial regulations which have been adopted. You will either have to give up the idea of furthering your studies, or resign from 'security'.

The colonial secretary is English. Maybe they think that 'security' is more important than education. You resign.

No one is in favor of your going. Not even your mother understands your reason for wanting to go. Perhaps she is afraid for you. But you have to go if you ever hope to escape from the quicksand of 'security'. You have to enter the world of insecurity. You leave.

As the airplane gradually rises above the green oasis in the sea, you look back longingly through the window and wonder: *how long will it be before I look again upon your shining white sands and emerald sea, beloved land of my birth? How long before I hear the lilting sound of the voices and the laughter of your beautiful Black daughters? How many long, long years before I feel the warmth of your life-giving sun, as I lie on your sandy beaches or listen to the sighing of the wind through the casuarinas, and hear the whisper of the wavelets as they caress the shore, singing a gentle lullaby in the silver moonlight. How long? How long?*

You look back at it until it fades from your sight. There is no answer.

The monotony of the flight of the propeller-driven Pan American plane soon lulls you to sleep and you only awaken when it lands in Bermuda for a short while. You descend the steps on to the tarmac with the shimmering heatwaves partially obscuring the view of the countryside in a country that has a special significance for you. Your father is buried there, somewhere. You rejoin the plane and take your seat. The flight begins again and you are on your way again to the land of milk and honey; a new land; a new people, a new life and an uncertain future.

Arrival

You arrive at Idlewild airport late in the evening. It is already dark. During the flight from the stopover in Bermuda your head is filled with thoughts and memories rekindled from the moment you stepped off the plane in that tropical island. In the lounge you look across the distant countryside, not seeing the people riding the motor scooters nor the beaches with their glistening white sand, trying to see the place where your father is buried, but not knowing in which direction to look.

He is buried out there somewhere. Where?

Daddy are there flowers on your grave?

You wish you could have seen his grave in that brief stopover.

Daddy, I promise I will return, someday, and put a lily by your head, and then I will see you again.

Now, when you land in New York at the end of that long journey, these thoughts are forced to leave your consciousness. The customs officer is curt and officially brusque. His uniform gives the impression of authority, or so it seems. You have the fried flying fish packed in the soda biscuit tin, all your mother could give you to send you on your way. Your solitary suitcase packed with the few clothes you have seems insignificant beside the many expensive ones of the other passengers. He makes you open the tin and the suitcase, and a feeling of helplessness, of nakedness, comes over you.

You are exposed. It seems that at that precise moment a thousand eyes are focused on you, daring you to raise your eyes above the fourth button of his uniform. When he has examined the contents he pushes the suitcase aside, unclosed. You pass inside with mumbled thanks, gathering your possessions which have now passed his scrutiny. You close your suitcase, clothing your nakedness, and only then dare raise your eyes. But among the thousands there is no one, no hand to guide, no familiar face or voice. No one.

You are among many but you are all alone. And that feeling of helplessness returns again. There is no one to meet you, no one to greet you, and this is your first time away from home. Fortunately, some kind person shows you how to get the bus to Penn Station, and how to get from there to the Bronx. You don't remember his name or face but you remember the anthurium lilies he is bringing to his wife.

It is early night when you reach the station. Instinct prevents you from accepting the offer from the man in the subway entrance who wants to help you with your suitcase. You are alone in New York.

Oh innocents, He sends his angels to guide you and watch over you. He wraps His arms around you. He shields you. You are there God.

You are riding on the noisy, dirty, squealing subway to the Bronx. The automatons with tired expressionless faces, shifting with the squealing wheels, remain imprinted on your memory even today. And when you get off at Prospect Avenue to start the long walk to 966, it is like the start of Jason's journey in search of the golden fleece. It is the start of your odyssey.

It is raining, the suitcase on your shoulder is heavy, and you have to make many stops before you reach the apartment building.

It is exciting. There is new music—the rhythms of the Puerto Ricans who are beginning to populate the area provide a link to your homeland. There is the wonderful sound of jazz coming from the Black bars. Jazz that you learned about and enjoyed whenever your friend who had come back from Columbia University played records on his hi-fi set. Jazz that you listened to in the early hours of the morning on your short-wave radio. Willis Conover and 'Music USA'. Now, as you stop for a few minutes and listen, it is like rain falling on the sun-parched ground. You absorb it.

You had read about Birdland and listened enraptured to the galloping riffs of Miles and Dizzy, and Bebop, and you were thrilled by the smooth, lilting, intricate and melodious harmonies of the Modern Jazz Quartet. Jazz! The jazz of Django and Getz and Oscar Peterson, and Billie, whose sounds were so different.

Now you are here. Now you can get your hunger satisfied. You can visit Birdland and see Bird and all the giants. You are in the Mecca of jazz. You can make your own pilgrimage. But Billie dies before you get to see her. She was murdered by dope. You never get to see her. You never get to see any of them.

As you walk up Prospect Avenue you smell odours different from any you have ever smelled before: the smell of barbecuing ribs, the smell of fruit you have never seen or tasted: grapes, peaches, plums, apples—eaten once a year at Christmas when they were brought to be sold at the exhibition* and when the Police Band played in the annual concert in the Park. And the lights. Those hundreds of flashing neon lights from the signboards on both sides of the street, and the hundreds of cars noisily rushing to and fro along the cobble-stone paved road. It all makes an indelible impression on you.

You find the apartment building. As you climb the few steps and open the door of the dirty building and enter, you smell Nelson Street: stale food, stale urine, unwashed bodies. You've left home, but home is still with you. Can you ever escape?

You walk the two flights of narrow stairs to a landing where there is hardly room for you and your suitcase, up to apartment 2A. You knock.

"Who is it?" The woman's voice, American, tinged with that accent which never seems to go away no matter how long a Bajan has left 'the rock'.

"It's me, your nephew," you answer.

"Wait, I'm coming."

And then you hear the sound of locks being undone. There are many locks. You have entered another world. In all your years back home, the doors were never locked. There was no need. Everyone trusted the other. Everyone looked out for the other. That was the age of innocence.

As the door opens you see your aunt for the first time. She is also seeing you for the first time, but it is as if you have known her all your life, through the 'parcel'. Every Christmas the parcel came. That is how you learned how Grape Nuts and Spam tasted. This is where you got your comic books and Boy's Annual to read and exchange with the other boys who also got parcels from their relatives in the America. She only knew that her brother, whom she had not seen or heard from in many years, had children in need. She sent the parcel every Christmas. You could depend on it.

Getting the parcel was an important aspect of Barbadian life. Everyone who had a relative or friend overseas looked forward to getting a parcel. Food, clothes and anything else which could be scraped together was put in the parcel to be sent home. And when it arrived, everyone shared in its contents, even neighbors and friends. The parcel was for everybody. The umbilical cord was never severed.

You walk through the door past the toilet and bath right by the door, and into the one-bedroom apartment, and you realize how poor she is also. Like many others who have come to this 'land of milk and honey' where the streets are 'paved with gold'.

She is of medium height and buxom, with a round face which shows wrinkles of worry and pain, but within which are kindly eyes. As she precedes you down the narrow corridors, she limps and wheezes constantly. She is happy to see you, but explains that she couldn't get to the airport to meet you. She couldn't get anyone to take her. It's a long way from the Bronx to Queens. She didn't have enough money to pay a taxi, and no one does anything for nothing here.

How different from back home.

The apartment is small. The window of the tiny kitchen and dining/living room look out on the bare red brick walls of the building across the narrow alley behind. There are no front windows. There is nothing to see but red brick walls. This is 'home' now.

You talk into the wee hours of the morning and later, when the sun has risen, you go across the street into the church and pray. The next day she takes you to the Port Authority Bus Station and you are on your way to Harpur College.

******

Your thoughts are jerked back to the present as a grunt and the creaking of bed springs indicate that your roommate has awakened. Even as you look at him he looks at you, stretches and, unexpectedly farts loudly. He reaches across the bed to his desk, picks up a pair of gold rimmed glasses, puts them on and says,

"Hi."

He is thin and anemic-looking, with a sharp pointed chin and the suggestion of freckles on pale cheeks. His eyes are gray beneath thin blond eyebrows, and thin arms end in thin fingers. He needs a shave. His ribs show when he throws off the blanket around his body. He is not wearing any pajamas, only boxer shorts. As he searches for the slippers with his feet, you notice that his toes are long and the toenails have dirt under them and need clipping. As his feet slip into the leopard skin slippers, he sits on the side of the bed and gives a loud sigh:

"Boy am I bushed! That was some party last night." His voice is heavy and almost nasal in its timbre.

"Yes." Your answer is non-committal, because you didn't go to the party. You arrived only that afternoon. You notice that he is older than the average student, almost your age, and you learn later that he is getting his college education through the G.I. Bill, having been in the army for some years.

Doors are beginning to slam, evidence that others are coming awake. Voices are raised in conversation which gradually becomes intelligible.

"Are you going to breakfast?"

"Yes," you answer.

"Well you had better hurry, or you will miss the bus."

"Okay."

You are not accustomed to dressing or undressing in front of another man, so you continue to sit and your glance strays back to the window. Only after he goes through the door on his way to the bathroom do you get up, gather your new towel, new tube of toothpaste and soap, and go down the corridor to the bathroom. The sinks in the new, fresh-smelling bathroom with its row of gleaming showers and shining tiles each have a customer washing, cleaning, shaving or soaping. They are all talking, but seemingly to no one in particular. So you go to the urinal. Even that is new to you. You urinate and press the gleaming chrome handle. The loud rush of water and the powerful suction which pulls the water startles and fascinates you. You press the handle again and watch the rush and disappearance of the water.

A sink becomes vacant, so you fill the place and begin to brush your teeth. You turn on the tap and put your hand to catch the water. The message to your brain is instantaneous, and your hand jerks back even before you are conscious of the action. You have turned on the hot water. This also is new and unfamiliar. The only times before that you have washed your face with hot water, were when you heated water in the saucepan to add to the bucket of cold water when you bathed back home, dipping it up with the cup made from the Ovaltine tin handled by the tinsmith, and pouring the water over your head. Now you have it with a twist of a handle.

The bathroom is finally free of all of them. You take your shower.

Your roommate is already dressed when you get back to the room. As you are dressing there is a knock on the door and a head and then a body appears around it.

"Hello, my name is Don, and I am the Proctor on the block." His voice is nasal. He has red hair and his face is rugged and handsome. When he comes inside you notice that he is big, over six feet tall, and his hand, when he shakes yours, has a strong grip. The plaid shirt and yellow slacks clash with the dirty sneakers on his feet.

"You are the new student from the Barbados Islands?" he asks.

"Yes, but it is not the Barbados Islands, just plain Barbados. It is only one island."

"Oh," he mumbles, slightly taken aback. "Anyhow, I am to take you to breakfast and then see that you are registered. You are a week late, so you missed orientation already. I'll meet you at the bottom of the corridor."

"Thank you," you answer as he turns and leaves. You finish dressing and join him and your roommate as they walk down the steep incline from the dormitory to the waiting bus. You carry your papers: the letters of admission and student visa, the bank draft for fifteen hundred dollars—all the money in your possession—and the smudged, tear-stained letter you wrote to your mother last night.

The yellow bus is filled with white people who are talking loudly as you approach. Now, as you step inside, there is silence. They look at you, you look at them. You alone are different. The bus jerks into movement as you and the Proctor sit together. The conversations gradually begin again and soon the noise in the bus is as loud as it was before you entered. You keep your head turned to the window and watch the scenery as it quickly unfolds.

The homes you pass are large, the highway is wide and

smooth—smoother and wider than any you have ever seen before you came to this country—and the lines of vehicles passing in either direction at high speeds seem never-ending. The bus turns a corner and passes over a wide river whose water flows slowly off into the distance. It eventually stops in a tree-lined avenue before a series of old-looking green and white buildings, prefabricated huts joined to an old colonial house.

At the entrance there are two large imposing white columns. You enter the building and walk down a long corridor, dimly lit in the early morning. Other corridors lead off from the main one you entered, and behind some of the open doors you see laboratories with various types of glassware and instruments, and others with strange, pungent smells. You are excited.

Breakfast is another new experience. After joining the line with other students, you take your tray and help yourself at the gleaming, stainless steel counter: two eggs, bacon, milk, toast, jam butter, tea. For the first time in your life you can eat as much as you want. More than that, you have a choice. Only two days ago you had to share one egg with your sister and brother, and you had to chase the hen off the nest in the fowl coop* in the yard to get it.

Registration is a continuous round of forms, cards, advisors, and rushing from one room to another. Eventually it is all complete. As you come back between the columns, you look up at them. Tall, straight, pointing to the sky, like the Royal Palms back home. A smile crosses your lips as you walk past the inscription on the granite stone at the entrance: *From breadth through depth to perspective.*

You take a deep breath and sigh loudly. You are a university student, a student at Harpur College of the State University of New York. A university student? A Harpur student? You are either crazy or an idiot. Only an idiot would enter university in a foreign country with money for only one semester. Only a twenty-five year old idiot would want to study in a system where he has no idea where to begin, or how it functions, where the standard is higher than he has ever known, and register for courses for which he has never even done the preliminary work. Only an idiot would do these things without adequate orientation, especially since he had not studied for eight years after leaving high school.

Only an idiot has that sort of ambition. Barbados produces many such idiots.

There is no turning back, you have crossed the Rubicon. You have to succeed. The die is cast.

PART III

Study

Seasons

Winter comes with a whisper, a fluttering of falling leaves of gold and red which leave branches stark naked in the sunlight. The snowflakes, light and pure in pristine whiteness, drift silently in the stillness of the windless afternoon. It comes suddenly during a Spanish class. One moment you are translating a passage from the Spanish novel 'Doña Perfecta', then you stop in mid-sentence and gaze at the marvelous whiteness of the soundless, drifting snowflakes which you are seeing for the first time.

The trees prepared themselves weeks before and you marveled at the changing colors of the leaves and the endless searching of the squirrels—cheeks bulging with nuts—scampering up the branches and into the tree trunks whose branches, stripped bare by the autumn winds, are now exposed in all their nakedness. The winds blow colder as the days grow shorter and your nose tingles with each cold breath you inhale.

The class ends and you rush outside. You hold your face to the sky and feel the soft caress of the snowflakes falling, disintegrating and disappearing, melting and leaving only a brief tingle where they have touched. You feel their gentle touch for only the briefest of moments, and then they are gone, melted into nothingness by the warmth of your skin. It is just the whisper of a touch, but a touch which leaves a feeling of inspiration at the wonder of their purity, their perfection, their briefness. In that briefness there is no permanence. Their purpose is to be and then to be no more. Like us. The snowflakes fall and die, and in their dying give life. They fall and melt and disappear and you revel in the newness. It is miraculous.

Many winters later you will curse those snowflakes when winter seems interminable and every winter season seems to last longer and forever, when the winds blow strong and the freezing ice cold winds cut through your clothes and into the innermost parts of your body. When your breath freezes and you walk on wooden feet with frozen toes, when your lips crack and bleed and when your tears form icicles on your cheeks and there is no respite.

But for now, it is nice.

You have gotten into college life fully as the weeks pass from early to late autumn, from your initiation as a freshman with all the accompanying hoopla, wearing the green and white 'beanie' and undergoing the indignities from the seniors. But you become one with your fellow students. You make friends and become known even though you are so much older than the vast majority of the others. But then you are so outstanding—only four members of the entire student body are Black, and you are the only one from overseas.

Working in the cafeteria washing dishes and pots and pans and mopping floors provides you with money for your fees and three meals a day. You get to know everybody and everybody knows you, but your best friends are a group of Jewish students from Brooklyn. You learn a lot about the Jews, their suffering and their foibles, their strengths and their weaknesses. You learn about the sacrifices the parents make for their children, their religion, and the strength of their faith. You see how they over-indulge and spoil their offspring, and you share in the care packages they bring when they visit at spring break. You learn to dance the hora and share the agonies of the 'Holocaust'. You realize that they are no different from your people.

You engage in the silliness of campus life: the 'panty-raids', and the practical jokes, like the time when those guys visit from one of the other universities and the boys in your hall decide to play tricks on them. Somehow they are able to convince the visitors that you are a headhunter from Africa who engages in a ritual before an altar every night, and they are invited to view the ceremony. You agree to go along with the prank. An altar is prepared on your desk, complete with candles, sheets and other paraphernalia. You dress for the occasion, with donations of attire from a number of your neighbors and place a knife in its scabbard on the center of the altar.

Close to midnight when the visitors are on their way, you kneel before the altar and begin your incantations. Out of the corner of your eye you see them creep into the room and sit in wonder on the edge of the bed. Your incantations—unintelligible mumblings of pure gibberish—get higher and higher until you suddenly grab the knife from the altar, pull it halfway out of the scabbard and with a loud shout, turn to the visitors and snap it back in the scabbard.

You have never seen people exit a room and disappear down a corridor so fast. Everybody in the room collapses on the floor with laughter. It is a good practical joke.

But maybe the joke is on you. You are Black, and the only one from overseas. Is that why you are a headhunter? Do they think that all Black people from overseas are headhunters?

College is fun, sometimes. College is serious most of the time. You have it tough that first semester. You are working many hours, taking too many credits, undertaking too many courses, and you don't understand the full meaning of the system of grade point average, cumulative average, the impact and effect of racial discrimination and prejudice, the marking system, or anything, without the benefit of guidance.

You nearly flunk out. But you learn and by the next semester your brain begins to function as it should and you do much better.

And then the winter's cold sets in with a vengeance. Winter! Cold-biting, muscle-shivering, nose-freezing, foot-numbing cold! And the winds, high winds blowing snow, freezing your breath, burning your cheeks and ears and any other parts that are exposed. And dirty, slushy, crunching snow on frozen snow-covered ground, walk-quickening cold, months-lasting cold. Heavy, hooded coat, fur-lined boots, COLD! COLD! COLD! COLD!

Running-between-classes cold. Bright-star-filled-night, full-moon-cloudless-sky cold, freezing cold. Spit-freezing cold. Sinus-valley cold. Snowball-fights-snowman-Christmas-and-New-Year's-night—cold. Unheated-apartment-in-December, in the Bronx—cold! Hot-water-in-a-bathtub-in-an-unheated-apartment-to-get-warm-before-jumping-into-bed—cold. Feet-bundled-up-in-heavy-fur-lined-coat-in-a-blanketless-bed—cold. God-damn-the-Superintendent!.... he-turned-off-the-heat—cold. Christmas-and-New-York-in-the-Bronx, all-day-in-a-movie-theatre-where-it-is-warm—cold.

COLD! COLD! COLD! Winter-Cold.

And then the songs of the birds begin. Spring comes, the snow melts, buds appear and so does a robin. And Beethoven's Eroica symphony evokes a desire to go and lie on the grass in the warming sun. Who wants to learn about plagel cadences when the sun is bright and warm, when the girls look like girls at last, when coats disappear and you realize that these girls have legs and breasts and bodies. And the tingle in your loins is the first sign of spring fever. It is a terrible affliction. Symptoms: a constant yearning, a desire to touch and to be touched accompanied by a quickening heartbeat, a desire to run outside, to jump in the rain and get soaking wet, to turn your face to the heavens and give thanks for release from winter.

And then it is summer. Your first year at University is over and you are still in. Nearly out, but still in. You are ecstatic. You are returning to be a sophomore. You will not have to go back home a failure. To return home a failure is worse than going to Glendairy Prison in Station Hill. That's what keeps so many native sons and daughters in exile—the thought of returning home a failure. They would rather die in exile; so many do.

But you are still in, and the sun is warm and the birds are singing and life is beautiful.

It is raining when your friend Gerry lets you out of his car at Yankee Stadium. You make the long trek up 169th Street and it is still raining when your aunt opens the door and greets you with a hug. She is happy to see you again and you talk for hours about your year at school and your plans for the future and she offers to try to get a job for you at the hospital where she works as a practical nurse.

That night you sleep blissfully on the folding cot in the corner of the living/dining room. Yours for summers and winter vacations.

You get the job at the Hospital for Chronic Diseases as a nurse's assistant. And the first place you work is in the psychiatric ward. It is there you learn to care for and about people who have so much less than you. You learn to take care of Mr. Cronin, all two hundred and eighty helpless pounds of blubber, and little Arnold, forty pounds of cerebral palsy, whose father is a doctor, and old Mrs. Birnbaum who, in her tortured brain would, or could only say "damn, damn, damn" all day, every day. Why?

And that summer you meet June again. June was your love in your innocent puppy love years. You used to walk with her to her home in Beckle's Road, after Sunday school at Bethel church. You were devastated when you heard she was going to 'the States' along with the rest of her family to join her father. You thought you would never see her again. Now she is here. You see her and talk to her. You go to Coney Island and the YMCA pool, and go to see My Fair Lady and you give her a George Shearing album.

You are in love again and love is renewed inside. You never tell her. In all the years later, when you come to Brooklyn to see her, you never tell her how you feel about her. Now she is a woman, desirable, gorgeous. Available?

And when she shows you in the subtle ways that women have of telling you that they too are interested, you hold back. You don't take the offering although you want to. When you hear many years later that she got married, you wish she hadn't.

That summer she takes you places: the beaches, Coney Island, the roller coaster, the bumper cars, and all the other rides. You have fun. It is idyllic in hot dusty dirty Brooklyn, amidst its winos, garbage-lined streets, fights, shootings, and the sirens. Sirens like in the Bronx.

As summer progresses you grow closer to your aunt. You come to understand the sadness in her eyes, her deep sense of loss and her loneliness. She has lived alone all these years, and later when she dies, she dies alone.

Her son, the only bright spot in her life, a student at Harrison college, the top secondary school in the island, dies while she is in 'the States'. She didn't even know his grave. She wasn't there when he died. She had left others to care for him while she sent money for his upkeep, like so many other parents did, so many other exiles. She wanted him to have a good education and upbringing. He got caught up in the wrong company, strayed, contracted a disease and died. She was alone. Always alone.

She crochets constantly, and she is good at it. She crochets everything: bedspreads, tablecloths, dresses, everything. Hours upon endless hours, on the subway, in her bed, on the bus, everywhere. It seems that every stitch is a link in the thread of her life, which she has to keep joining for fear it would end. There seems to be desperation in her crocheting.

You try to show her that you love her and try to fill her need, you try to be the son she never had—to be a son to her, what he could not be. You could never fill that void. She never stops crocheting until finally the thread ends. She dies. She never returns home, to a home she no longer knows. She is exiled forever.

Prospect Avenue is in Spanish Harlem, which is a study in

schizophrenia. There is always activity, always noise, and there are always people on the streets, a conglomerate mixture of faces, always hurrying. There are no smiles, just expressionless faces. And in one block there is everything: between 164th and 165th street and Prospect Avenue there is everything.

You come down the steps of the apartment building and look around. On the left side there is the hotel, with a constant stream of 'guests' without luggage, and always couples. And in the basement of the hotel, three steps below the street level is the bar. And on the right side there is the funeral parlor: '...and the Lord said unto my Lord sit thee at my right hand', and nextdoor is the flower shop, flowers for the living and the dying and the dead. On the opposite side is the church where you prayed, and nextdoor is the pawn broker, and the supermarket, and the movie house, the shoemaker, the laundry and the barbershop. Across the street there is the barbecue house and the beauty parlor and the grocer with his fruit all over the sidewalk. In that one block, on either side of the cobblestone street along whose length runs the electric buses, is everything needed to survive. You could live and die and never leave the block.

The numbers runners are everywhere. Every day someone gets arrested for the numbers, but everybody plays the numbers secretly. The cops play the numbers. They get them from the pimps who get them from the whores, who get them from their clients and on and on. They get them and give them to the runners who collect the slips, the money, and make the payments and get arrested. Everybody's hopes are pinned on the numbers and the hope of 'hitting it big' and getting away from the block. None of them do. And there are also the men selling pamplets: Muhammed Speaks, seeking converts to the Muslim faith and attempting to sell another world to the black man, another Marcus Garvey, another Father Divine, another way to salvation that is not a 'white' way. And people hurry by as if ashamed to be seen with them.

But at night it is different. The day-people go to bed and the night-people come out. Spanish Harlem becomes vibrant; it comes alive as if from a deep sleep. Hundreds of lights from hundreds of neon signs flash on and off continuously, and the cars rush to and fro, their wheels rumbling over the cobblestones, and the sirens scream all hours of the night: sirens of fire engines, sirens of police cars, sirens of ambulances. They never stop, and as you lie in bed you can tell which one is answering the call as they hurry past the building, their noise blending with the rumble of the subway passing on the overhead tracks that curl around the building behind your room.

The music never stops either. The Puerto Rican rhythms from a hundred record players blending with the sounds of the streets into a cacophony with its own beat, its own sound, pulsating, unending, comforting. Reliving for them a taste of home. And the women, all types and sizes and shapes, and colors—teasing, taunting, promising, withholding. And the Puerto Rican men dressed in their rented tuxedos, shoes shining. In their shiny cars going to pick up their women—to go where? Downtown.

The horns of the cars in the wedding procession blend with the squeal of the subway overhead. Peacocks strut, ablaze with color. The Matadors, each in his 'suit of lights' entering the arenas to meet the 'cows'. But who is playing whom? For whom are the olés and who delivers the coup de grâce? The pushers? The gangs? The drunks? The junkies, once innocent children, beloved of their mothers? They all fall in the sand to be dragged away, out of the arena, gored, dying, or already dead, their arms a legacy of their struggles. And the sirens scream as they take them away and other matadors take their place.

Spanish Harlem never sleeps. Like Nelson Street. Like a heart it pumps constantly. It keeps everyone alive, but it is diseased and spreads its toxin into every corner, through the arteries of its streets, into the dark recesses of its alleys, up on the roofs, and on the fire escapes, in the rooms of 'walkups' and cold unheated rooms. The toxin spreads: drugs, prostitution, corruption, vandalism, dirt, disease, poverty, murder. You smell it and taste it and live it in Spanish Harlem.

And as you see it you see Nelson Street and you know that even here, three thousand miles away, in the 'land of milk and honey', where the streets are 'paved with gold', it is no different.

Summer vacation ends and you go back to school to begin a year which is to change your thinking and your life forever. It is a year which is to change the country and the world, forever. It is a year which is to change the Black American forever. It is a year that is to change the Black man forever. It is the start of the Civil Rights movement. It is the start of Martin Luther King's journey to martyrdom. It is the year of your second birth.

You enter fully and with enthusiasm into your scholastic endeavors, and you begin to understand, everything. You see the news on television, you experience, and for the first time fully understand, what it is to be Black.

Back home, discrimination and prejudice never impacted like this. You had your circle and stayed within it. You knew discrimination existed, but you ignored it, because you were ignorant to the implications of the mental slavery and its shackles to which you were still bound. Your consciousness never reached the level it is here. Here it is different. You are made aware. Your Blackness is a yoke, a heavy yoke, which requires more strength than you have to lift it. It is around your neck forever. You are in the stocks. You are helpless, exposed. You feel your Blackness.

You see your Blackness in your grades, and realize your Blackness in the comments of some of your professors. "If I used to give A minus, you would get an A minus, but I only give A or A plus, so I have to give you a B plus plus." And you need that A for your grade point average.

You are aware of your Blackness in the barber shop. He doesn't refuse to cut your hair, but when he is finished, he knows that you will never come again. You buy a cap.

You see your Blackness in the South. In Birmingham, Atlanta, North Carolina, Arkansas, and Mississippi.

You know your Blackness, and you are aware. You are part of it and it is part of you. For the first time you see your blackness in the mirror. You cannot escape. Your feelings are determined by your Blackness. Your reactions are determined by your Blackness.

You march in the picket line outside Woolworth, caught in the tide of awareness and militancy and pride, pride in the sign you carry as you march on the sidewalk outside the store. Your sign is your banner, your standard. It represents your transition. Your spirit soars and you are unafraid, even though you should be afraid. There is resentment and jeers, and spittle, and curses, but you are proud. You know how your brothers and sisters in the South feel, for you can now identify with them. You would die before you let that standard fall to the ground.

You once carried the flag of your Scout Troop, and you remember the pride with which you shined the brass emblem on the flag staff the night before, so that it gleamed in the afternoon sun. You held it high and marched ahead of your troop to the Thinking Day* service, marched to the drums and martial music of the Royal Barbados Police Band, marched with your head held high, for it was a great honor to be chosen to carry the flag.

This placard you now hold high is your flag, although there is no martial music, no band, just the singing: "We shall overcome."

And in Birmingham, Birmingham, Birmingham, Alabama, Alabama, Alabama, the dogs bit, and the hoses wet, and the cops beat, and the blood flowed, and the bombers bombed and the church fell, and the children died, and the parents cried.

And Bull Connor was king. And King prayed, and the people stood at the monument before Lincoln together. And King spoke of his dream. And the dream came true, almost.

Time passes quickly when classes start again. Days flow into nights of study, and work, into labs, and work, a continuous round of activities which you now begin to enjoy. There is so much to learn. A new vista appears before you and you see a new world. You learn to question, to probe, to analyze, to argue with strength, to be objective, to inquire, to search, to be critical, to think independently. Everything appears like a kaleidoscope before you. Ruth Benedict, de Tocqueville, Adam Smith, Milton, Aristotle, Virgil, Plato, Socrates, Kant, Donne, Dostoyevsky, Faulkner, Marx, Engel, and so many more, all writers. Chemistry, Biology, Zoology, Microbiology, Comparative Anatomy, Physiology, Embryology. Experiments, examinations, seminars, discussions, arguments.

There is so much to learn, so much to enjoy, so much to cover in four years. Work, work, study, study. There is constant activity. Examination merges into examination, spring into summer, into autumn, into winter, into spring, until it is over. It seems to pass so quickly.

And then there are no more requirements to be filled, no more examinations to be taken, no more seminars to be presented. It is over.

Graduation is here. You have triumphed. But there is no one from home to share your triumph, no one to share your joy, no one to see you in your cap and gown.

Only your Jewish friends.

The parents come and proudly hold their parties, and you are invited. There is pride and joy in their conversations: "My son has been accepted to Upstate Medical School. Isn't that fantastic? My son the doctor. Come and take a picture with your mother."

"Where are you going?" They ask you. "Oh I'll be staying here. I am going to study Medical Technology. I'll be here for at least another year."

You are not going home. Or are you at home? Where is home? Home is this place you know now. You fit in, you are accepted, and you are known. Home is here. But home is somewhere else. Here is where you want to be. That other place is fading from your memory, but not your heart. Something keeps you tied to that far off place. Is this what happens to every exile?

At Mike's party you are particularly sad. He has become one of your best friends during your years of study. He is Jewish, and you have had many long discussions and arguments about zionism, judaism, racism, literature, music, all sorts of topics. You have discussed politics, people, slavery the holocaust, and life in general. Many of your arguments were never resolved, and your logic was always at odds with a type of intransigence in his attitude, especially when you discussed slavery. He never agreed with you that slavery was worse than the holocaust.

It is difficult to argue the problems of Blackness and get white people to understand. You can only understand if you have suffered. Perhaps from his perspective it is as difficult to explain judaism and zionism to those who are not Jewish.

The subject of Jewish settlement of the 'promised land' was a topic which produced one of the most heated arguments between you, eventually involving a large number of students. Once more it was a discussion of the contrasts and comparisons between the holocaust and slavery, and the results of these events on the psyche of the people affected, and the generations who follow.

"I tell you that no other people have suffered like the Jews. We have been down-trodden from Biblical times, and we suffered even more in the last World War." Mike said one wintry evening while you were seated in the lounge after an exhausting day of lectures and labs.

"But the Blacks suffered even more, we were slaves. Everything was taken away from us, even our culture. At least you still had your faith. The slaves were made to feel that they had nothing, not even faith in their Gods, in their heritage, culture or traditions. Everything was taken or beaten out of them. They had to conform to the whims and fancies of the new masters; take their names, their culture, even their God."

You were in the right mood for the battle you knew was coming.

"The Israelites were slaves too, but God took us out of Egypt, and gave us the Promised Land."

This concept had bothered you for a long time since you had read the Bible through completely during the weeks you were ill with chicken pox. You had become 'conscious', and spent a lot of time analyzing the Exodus and the role Moses played in this movement of the Hebrews from Egypt.

"How could a nebulous being, an imaginary concept, give something tangible? The scriptural writings have been doctored to suit the occasion. The recordings of the journey to the promised land, as written, clearly indicate that the entire episode was simple politics."

This perplexed him.

"What do you mean politics? This was a historical event. Moses fought for the Jewish slaves. You can't maintain it was politics."

"That's exactly what I am talking about. Moses was a political opportunist, a power seeker who saw the chance to become what he could never become living in Pharaoh's court."

He seemed more confused, and it showed in his face and voice.

"I don't understand what you are saying." He said, his brow furrowed.

"Okay, let's examine it logically. Moses was taken from the river by Pharaoh's daughter, and raised in the court as her own. As Pharaoh's adopted son, he would have received the best education and teachings. He would have been privy to all the secrets of the court magicians, who would have been his teachers. In addition, he would have observed all the intrigue and machinations that took place at court. Do you follow me so far?"

"Yes." He said hesitantly. He wasn't sure where you were coming from.

"But Moses could never become the supreme power, a Pharaoh, because he was of Jewish heritage. He could never be a leader of the Egyptians. His ultimate ambition was to be a leader, but this could never happen as long as he was among the Egyptians. He wanted power—the power of a Pharaoh. He saw that the Jews who were in bondage at the time were leaderless, despondent, and desperate. Hebrews were not really slaves. They were immigrants who were a source of cheap labor, exploited by the Egyptians. He saw the opportunity to foment an uprising, organized a strike of the brick makers, and challenged the authority of the Pharaoh."

"That seems logical, but according to our history, it's not accurate." Michael interjected.

"It's just that no one has looked at the Exodus from a political perspective. No one has really looked at the politics of the Bible or the political machinations that were exhibited by the kings, priests and politicians of the Bible. Everyone has only looked at it in terms of the freeing of the Hebrews. No one has looked at the political intrigues which must have taken place."

He was beginning to see the direction in which your arguments were heading. He was not convinced.

"What about the miracles which took place to force Pharaoh to release the children of Israel?"

"They can be explained as natural phenomena, which Moses exploited to his benefit."

"What about the incident with the serpents?"

"Those were simple magic tricks which Moses would have learned as part of his tuition at court. When he realized that the opportunity was available to take advantage among the Jews, and Pharaoh's grief at the loss of his son, he seized it.

Moses was a revolutionary. He eventually got the upper hand of Pharaoh and led the Jews out of Egypt, but the interesting thing is that he had no idea where he was taking them."

Mike became very flustered.

"What do you mean by that? He led them to the Promised Land, Israel?"

"Ah, that's where you are wrong. He had no idea where he was going or where the promised land was. He gave the Hebrews the hope that they were going to a better place—the promised land, but when they left Egypt and crossed into the desert, he had no idea which way to turn. That's why they wandered in the desert for so many years. Under normal circumstances that journey should only take about eleven days, but Moses took forty years. As a matter of fact there was not even a place called Israel. According to the scriptures, Jacob 'wrestled' with God all night, and in the end God called him 'Israel' because he had struggled so mightily. After that his offspring were called the children of Israel. Israel the person, not a place."

"What about the Ten Commandments? What about the burning bush?" interjected one of the other students who had become interested in the discussion and who crowded around, listening.

"Use your common sense," you said with some tension in your voice, "who witnessed that event? Moses was on the mountain alone. What better way to get acceptance for his edicts than to say that they were given directly by the hand of God, carved in granite? The Pharaoh was the initiator of the concept of one God; the Sun God. This concept had obviously made an impression on Moses. Prior to his sojourn on the mountain, there was turmoil in the Jewish camps where the newly freed tribes went back to their old ways. They went back to the worshipping of idols in an atmosphere of debauchery and general lawlessness. Moses was losing control. The Ten Commandments are nothing but a basic constitutional outline—the first attempt at a written constitution and rules for self-government. They were in essence a code of conduct by which the Jews should govern themselves. A code of conduct applicable to all. In addition, by stating that they were carved by the hand of God himself reinforced Moses' concept of a single God, a concept which was new to the Jews."

The number of students crowding around was quite large. You were so engrossed in the argument and topic that you were only vaguely aware of their presence. They began to voice differing opinions.

Mike still did not accept your argument.

"But you can't deny that God gave the promised land to the Jews," one of the students stressed.

"Okay, you tell me that He gave, note the word gave, this land. Are you saying that He physically defined boundaries, set line marks, and that a map of the area appeared out of the heavens?" You asked derisively.

"Of course that didn't happen," he responded.

"Well then, how can you say that He gave the promised land to the Jews? All that happened was that after years of wandering in the desert they finally came across a fertile area, and decided that this was where they would settle. They claimed the land as theirs, making the spurious assertion that it was given by God. The rights of the inhabitants were trampled, and even today, the claim is still made that the land belongs to the Jews. In reality it doesn't."

This statement resulted in general uproar in the lounge. Loud arguments, pro and con, started, with each side loudly defending its position.

Mike looked at you. He was angry, very angry.

"You don't like Jews very much do you?" He said, his eyes blazing.

You looked at him directly, your gaze as fixed as his.

"It has nothing to do with not liking Jews. It is necessary to look at things objectively, from all sides. That is what we are learning here at university. We must analyze and not accept unquestioningly everything we are shown, read or even taught. All I am doing is trying to analyze the claims of inheritance of the promised land from a different perspective. You are my friend, and we must be able to discuss and argue, and still be friends. You don't have to agree with me, but don't be annoyed with me for my opinions. They might be wrong, but they are mine nevertheless, and you have to show me by cogent argument and facts where I am wrong. You have to convince my by the force of your argument and facts and bring me over to your side."

You were conciliatory. His anger slowly dissipated.

"You're right." He said this very quietly, and held out his hand. You took it in yours and as he gripped yours, you knew that this friendship was lasting. The arguments continued for some time after the two of you had left the lounge; Mike to go to the dormitory, and you to your room at the YMCA.

Now, as the two of you stand next to each other on the balcony of the Howard Johnson Hotel where the graduation celebrations are being held, you gaze across the river to the campus. There it is, serene, silent, uninhabited. Your own Egypt from which you have separated, each of you a tribe setting out to find your own 'promised land'; to part, maybe never to see each other again.

It is time to go and, as you embrace, you know that you are probably seeing each other for the last time in this life.

"It was good to have known you." He says, and you see the tears in his eyes.

"Same here. We learnt a lot from each other in these few years, and I shall never forget your kindness and help."

The lump in your throat makes it difficult to speak.

"Maybe we'll meet sometime," he says quietly.

"No. We have to be realistic. Soon you will be a doctor, with a thriving practice in Queens. I will probably go back home, sometime, but I don't think we will ever see each other again."

You reach out and shake hands warmly. His parents embrace

you as you bid them goodbye, and without a backward glance, you walk down the stairs.

You enter your desert, to seek your own promised land....

PART IV

Return

Independence

You return to your homeland without the feeling of nostalgia which had engulfed you on your departure five years earlier. Instead, it is the same feeling you had when you landed in New York. You feel that you have come to a strange land.

You return without fanfare, without the welcoming sounds of the conquering hero's martial music although you have conquered, or the glad rejoicing for the prodigal son who had returned from his exile in the land of debauchery.

You return to a changed landscape, a changed land, a changed people with changed attitudes, and feel the trepidation, the momentary terror of a stranger in unfamiliar territory, a seemingly strange land.

The customs officer in the arrival shed is as brusque as the one you met when you landed at Idlewild Airport five years earlier. He is as brusque as if you were a stranger. But maybe you are.

You want to go home. But you can't. Where you want to go to isn't home. You are home. But it doesn't feel like home.

You are in a strange land, walking streets you don't recognize, seeing people you don't know, faces which are strange even though they are Black faces, buildings you have never seen before. Feeling lost, feeling lonely, home.

You write many letters back 'home' to the hospital where you had undergone your training, where you have friends. You want to go back. You want to rejoin the 'Summer Savoyards' and sing Gilbert and Sullivan again. You want to go to the lake and swim in the icy water, feeling its chill on your skin as you swim among the reeds, even though here you have the warmth of the sun and can listen to the gentle sound of the waves rolling in to the shore.

Back 'home' you have friends. Here, your former friends have themselves become exiles in other lands. You can't get back 'home'. You are in the middle. In limbo.

Back 'home' you were not at home, you were an immigrant. Your feelings are those of confusion. You can't get settled. You are home, but you are nowhere. Nothing seems right. Nothing is as it was before, as you remembered it.

Then you realize that when an exile leaves his home, he takes a moment in time with him which remains until his return. But that moment has been replaced as the country has moved forward. That moment must be relinquished, or the exile will find no peace, no rest from his longing for the past.

Then one of your friends from school days introduces you to membership in his cricket club, and you are accepted. Gradually, through the passage of time, the wounds of loneliness begin to heal and as surroundings resume their familiarity, you assimilate.

Reality gains the ascendancy, and 'home' becomes home. That other home fades from your consciousness, with only the occasional memory, reminding you that there was another home.

Then you get involved in what is taking place in the island. The island is undergoing a transition.

The trauma caused by the demise of the West Indies Federation*, that exercise and attempt to create unity out of diversity without preparing the people, without educating them into the nuances of unity, was slowly and haltingly healing. But the disappointment among many sectors in many of the islands caused a bitterness which led to further disharmony.

An attempt was made to create a mini-federation out of

the rubble; after the famous statement from one of the larger islands: 'One from ten equals naught.' This statement by one of the former federalists may have been the catalyst.

They tried to create a mini-Federation out of the rubble; a Federation of the 'little eight'*. But insularity, political selfishness, and crass stubbornness stimulated the desire, in some quarters, for Barbados to withdraw from that proposal and become Independent, set in.

The island then entered a decisive phase in its future. It entered a period of intense political activity which saw the birth of a new political party, new alliances, and fresh elections. It saw the emergence of a group of young, brilliant, legal minds; the 'Under Forties'*, who joined the battle along with the Barbados Labor Party, arguing in favor of Independence within a Federation of the smaller islands. The Democratic Labor Party favored Independence alone, and the sides were arrayed against each other. The battle was joined.

The Independence debates, mass meetings, arguments, and discussions, at street corners, in rum shops, in the 'bus stand cabinet'* and a hundred other places, became the focus. The Pro-Independence supporters won the debate, and gave the Democratic Labor Party a mandate to sever ties with the 'mother country'. It received a mandate to disentangle the island from England's 'apron strings', to launch out into the deep, on its own.

It rained heavily at the Garrison Savannah that night. And then, out of the darkness, at the witching hour, it was born. The Broken Trident unfurled. And amid the mud and slush, and sodden ground, the hush was loud in the stillness of the windless night, and then the shouts of a hundred thousand voices broke the stillness, and they heard an anthem. Ours, and no one else's. It was ours, in praise of us. Made by us, for us. It was OURS!

"These fields and hills, beyond recall, [were] now our very own."

This land, this place, this island home, this INDEPENDENT land, was now ours. We celebrated, we sang, we laughed, and in our exuberance almost overwhelmed the Supremes. This exuberance was misinterpreted by some, and the riot police were on standby. But it was only the exuberance of freedom.

We understood how we must have felt those many years earlier, when the chains were removed from our wrists and ankles. This was the exuberance which we felt when we no longer had to labor at 'massa's' behest. This was the exuberance we felt when we were emancipated from slavery, when we could shout to the rooftops: 'Massa day done! Done! Done! Done!'

Now we were free from our colonial massas. We were proud of our heritage, and our land, and we showed this in our exuberance. We entered the world of nations, equal with the biggest and the smallest. INDEPENDENT! *'Friends of all, satellites of none.'* Free! And Independent.

And then a different kind of emigration took place. The prospect of independence raised for some of the white people on the island the specter of Black domination. Political, not economic. And many of them could not accept that. Rumors were spread about what and what would happen once independence was achieved. And they emigrated (fled? escaped?) to Australia and New Zealand, as far away as it was possible to get, taking their (our?) money with them, almost causing an economic collapse in the fledgling nation.

But the island and the people stood strong, and got stronger with Independence. It grew quickly.

And some of them came back many years later like loopy dogs*, but some are still there, wanting to come back. They also feel the longings of the exile, for they too are exiles. They too long for the warm nights when the moon is full and shines like day, and the soft breezes rustle the sugar cane stalks, and the air is sweet with the smell of boiling sugar cane juice, and the perfume of the 'lady of the night' which is carried by the wind, which laughs with happiness as it blows across the land.

This land was now ours.

Then the energy of a people long held in check by dependency burst forth. We created our own: our own beat, our own music, our own heroes. We had Garfield, and Charlie, and Wes, and Conrad, and Jackie Opel, and the Draytons, and Emile and the Merrymen, and Wendy, and Spouge*. They were ours, no one else's. The music was ours.

There was Pride. We challenged the world at cricket. We showed them that we were not afraid to take on the world. We were a nation, proud and Independent.

Mother

You stop your car by the side of the road and watch the figure approaching in the distance. As you sit there in the midday Sunday sun beads of perspiration gradually form and, drop by drop, fall to your lap as the heat in the car increases.

As you watch the figure gets larger, but it seems that an interminably long time has passed, and yet she seems not much closer. Her steps are slow, almost painful, although it is clear even from this distance that the slowness is caused by the effect of time. Every now and then she stops to pick up something from the road, sometimes putting it into the old handbag she carries on her arm. Step by slow step she approaches, and as she gets nearer the silver of her matted hair shines brighter in the sun. Soon you can see the wrinkles on her cheeks, even see her mouth moving as she talks to herself, to God, or to someone else inside her head. Her body is thin and covered by a dress which reaches beneath her knees. The stockings are full of holes, some of which run into the slippers which drag on the ground with each step. Her thin shoulders and arms are covered by a light blue knitted wool sweater, which she wears even in the broiling sun.

But it is her eyes which attract. They are bright beneath the thin graying eyebrows, and seem to see everything, burning with a fire which the years have not dimmed. And even though age has bowed her shoulders, there is pride in her bearing, which speaks volumes for her youth.

As you sit in the hot car you do not realize that tears have joined the drops of perspiration, so that it is difficult to tell which drops are which. This woman, this queen, this gem whose slow steady steps, whose silver gray hair covers her intelligence, her pride, her hopes, her memories, whose strength has been sapped by the burdens of the years and by the struggles against insurmountable odds, who sacrificed her pride rather than her children, who suffered that they might have, is a mirror image of so many others in this island. This lady walks in the midday sun after worshipping her God, in whom she has such faith even in her darkest days, her dream filled days, her sleepless nights, her days and nights of hallucinations, her hunger-filled weeks, even in her moments of loneliness and despair, even in those days when the only thing she had to give to her children was her love for them and a lesson in love for their fellow man, God, and themselves. Even then her faith in her God did not falter. This queen was yours.

And as she passes your car, the love and tenderness you feel for her makes you reach out to touch your mother.

Hercules, in his labors in the Aegean stables, eventually triumphs and is suitably rewarded. For a woman to be able to raise children in this island in the years of your childhood without the presence of a male figure-head, or financial assistance from a source other than that provided by a job as a maid, makes Hercules' labors seem trivial.

When your father died, she made the decision not to give you a stepfather. She taught you everything she knew—how to make do with what you have with contentment.

There was no electricity. You studied by the light of the kerosene lamp, or the lighted wick floating on a bowl of cooking oil. She taught you to love yourself, love your fellow man, and to be honest and truthful. She disciplined, not with abuse or unnecessary force, but with her voice, and by example. She gave you ambition and drive, and taught you that there was nothing to be ashamed of in being poor, because of circumstances over which you have no control. But she also taught you that there was no need to wallow in self-pity. The most important lesson you learned was that education was a way to escape the trap of poverty.

The struggle over the years finally broke her.

For years after you can only watch in pain and love as she goes through the hallucinations and mood swings, and withdrawal. Love kept her at home. Love succeeded.

She is old now, but each time you see her you remember, and you thank God for her.

"She went to Panama, you know..." with her mother who went to meet her husband who worked on the Panama Canal. She used to speak about it sometimes, but each time she remembered, she pushed it back into her subconscious. The memories seemed too terrible, haunting her like some dream she wanted to forget. Occasionally something would slip out. Like the terror she felt on her journey in the boat, where the portholes were so far beneath the water that she could see the fishes. These would be replaced by memories of her life in the Canal Zone, where she went to High School.

"It was just like Queen's College, you know…" she would say. And then the veil would be pulled in front of the window of her mind again.

Sometimes you could see behind the window a mirror and a reflection of a young, sensitive, ambitious, proud, loving woman with high hopes and dreams, all dashed before they bloomed and ripened. Crushed as the half-ripe mango when it falls to the ground; crushed by everyone who passes. All her dreams crushed by poverty.

In all these years she does not speak much about herself, and even today, to you, she is a stranger, locked in the prison of her feelings.

Sarah

She walks across the compound as you stand on the balcony talking with the chief accountant. You are immediately struck by a number of things. She walks with an upright, almost regal bearing. There is a softness to her features which enhances the beauty of her face, and her steps are firm and confident. She stops and speaks to one of her contemporaries. You can't keep your eyes off her. The conversation with the chief accountant is no longer registering. You decide on the spur of the moment that you have to get to know her.

"Louis, who is that lady?" you ask, turning to the chief accountant as she enters the building.

"That is Sister Smith, a senior nursing sister. She is one of the best we have in this hospital."

"I'd like to meet her." You are surprised at your own boldness. Since your return to the island you had been so busy adjusting to your 'new home' that you had not established any romantic associations. Now all of a sudden your hormones spring into action. This beautiful lady stimulates your romantic instincts. You have to get to know her.

The opportunity comes some weeks later. The annual dance of the Nurses' Association is scheduled for the upcoming weekend. Like all those dances it is to be held at the Nurses' home and it will be a formal affair. It might be the opportunity to fulfill a life-long ambition.

As a young man growing up nearby, you had often passed Wellington Street and stopped to listen to the music emanating from those dances. You had often stood on the steps of one of the houses and looked through the window at the beautiful women in their elegant gowns moving gracefully over the dance floor in the arms of their partners as the music of the Percy Green band or the Arnold Meanwell orchestra, on the platform above the dance floor, accompanied the swaying dancers. At that time you wished that you could have been among that group of seemingly privileged persons; only a certain class of people became nurses, the best-educated women, and later a few men. Nurses were special. They were protected. They lived in the nurses' home, were allowed to go home when they were not in training, but had to sign out when they left the premises, and sign back in when they returned. Boyfriends had to meet them outside the precincts of the hospital and stay outside when they brought them back. It was a privilege to be loved by a nurse, and to be invited to a dance at the nurses' home.

Dancing was an important social activity. It was important to be able to dance well, to be able to execute the graceful steps of the waltz and foxtrot, but also to be able to dance to calypso and do the jerk-waist*. A young man exposed himself to ridicule not only from his male friends, but invited ostracism by the women he might ask to dance with him. You avoid this by getting some books on dancing from the library, marking out the steps on the floor and carefully putting your feet in the marks while listening to records on the wind-up gramophone your mother has somehow obtained from a second hand shop in Baxters Road. Practice at dances in Queens Park for sixty cents admission, and more formal affairs at the Drill Hall, the entertainment centre of the Barbados regiment, lighten your feet so that you are now a more confident and better dancer. You don't need to fear ridicule or refusal.

You do not need to seek an invitation to the dance. You are a member of the hospital team and it is easy to get a ticket. You dress carefully and leave early for the short drive to the nurses' home. You arrive early and that suits you perfectly. It gives you time to survey the scene and the atmosphere. It is a beautiful night. The moon is full and the soft sound of the orchestra provides a perfect background to the calm and peace of the night. A few couples are on the floor and you spend a few minutes watching them. You don't see Sister Smith and you wonder if she is going to be there. You have come there specifically to see her without knowing whether she is even going to be there. You are trusting in the 'powers that be' to accede to your wishes, for you wish her to be there. You have been thinking a lot about her since you first saw her. You have even made enquiries about her, for her face and the picture you have imprinted on your mind of this tall, graceful woman, her white cap perched on her perfectly coiffed hair, are with you constantly. She is well respected and is very careful about her acquaintances. She is a prize. You have gone out of your way to position yourself to see her many times since that first time, admiring her from a distance. You will her to be at the dance, you want—need—to talk to her and get to know her.

You never even consider your presumption in assuming that she might even be interested in you, or whether or not she has a boyfriend. All you are interested in is getting to know her. Your sojourn up north has infused you with a self-confidence that surprises even you at times. You identify the objective and pursue it with single-minded focus, overcoming any obstacles that seem to get in the way.

She is dressed in a lovely evening gown; pink, with an off-the-shoulder blouse of an iridescent aquamarine colour. She is gorgeous. She wears no makeup, but there is a touch of lipstick that blends into the colour of her skin. Your heart skips a beat when she enters the room. She walks over to the chairs placed at strategic points around the dance floor, and greets a friend, one of the other nursing sisters. She is graceful when she walks and exudes charm in her speech.

They talk for a few minutes. You wait until she stops speaking and looks around the room. You approach, and you introduce yourself.

"May I have this dance?" You ask.

She looks briefly at her friend who gives her a wink and slight nod of her head. She comes into your arms as the orchestra begins a waltz. She comes into your arms easily, and even though she is slightly taller than you are, it is no impediment. She is a beautiful dancer. The floor is smooth—it is customary at these dances to either wax the floor or sprinkle powder on it so that it is easy for a good dancer to glide effortlessly across it, but hazardous for the uninitiated. The music ends and you reluctantly let her go, but you know that you will have many more dances together, and you do. You dance with her until it is time for the dance to end. It is almost three in the morning. You part reluctantly, but you know how to reach her.

That is the beginning. You fall in love. She is what you have wanted all your life. She is fun, tender, loving, sophisticated, smart, talented and has the qualities of humanity, understanding, sympathy, empathy and courtesy that make those born to be nurses, nurses. She returns your love and you want to show yours in the extreme. You make plans for marriage, but fate intervenes and your hopes are dashed to the ground. You ask her to marry you. She consents. You begin to make preparations for that eventful day. You are happier than you had ever been before, even though you are still relatively innocent.

And then the gods intervene. You are chosen to leave the island to pursue a course overseas. Plans for marriage have to be put on hold. The God of envy in others—those who feel that you are not suited for each other—intervene. Doubts are planted in her. The God of ambition intervenes on your side and pushes you to think of pursuing other studies when you return. It also conspires to send her on a course overseas as soon as you return. By the time she returns, it is over. Doubt and suspicion have been instilled in her head by those who don't want you together, and openly demonstrate this.

You are devastated when she returns your ring, for you really love her deeply, sincerely and everlastingly, and even today you still have that love and often rail at the gods for tearing you apart. But they have their way. You recover and then your new, changed circumstances mean that you make that fateful decision to journey north once again. Further study and work take you away to Canada to start a new life, in a new country with new friends and marriage.

Sarah comes into your life during that transition period.

You are seated in the small restaurant on Broad street having lunch. It is the middle of the hot weather period just before the hurricane season. The island is beginning to get over the euphoria of Independence and beginning to see growth in the economy brought on by the implementation of Operation Beehive, the thrust toward industrialization and away from the plantation economy that has held the island and people in bondage for over two hundred years. Overseas investors are being encouraged by the government to set up factories, and are being encouraged to open for business in a country with well-educated, skilful people, liberal tax policies and fiscal incentives, and they are responding. Affluence is growing, and subsidiary businesses are beginning to appear.

You look up as a soft voice asks:

"Can I sit with you?"

"Of course." You say.

She places her tray with her lunch on the table and sits in the vacant seat across from you. The restaurant is full and this is one of the few available chairs. You don't object; it would be discourteous. And you are glad for the company. You have been slightly depressed after your failed love affair and it is good to have female company. Most of the days you eat lunch alone or with one of the boys from the club.

She is good-looking, with a small face and head atop a well proportioned body. Her eyes are sad though, as if she is worried about something and needs to talk about it. You give her that opportunity.

"You look as if you are worried about something," you say after she sits and you have introduced yourself. "What is your name?"

"My name is Sarah," she says quietly, not eating the food on her plate. "Yes, I am worried." She seems relieved that the opportunity to unburden her mind has presented itself.

"My son is in hospital and they can't seem to find out what's happening with him. He has had fever for the past couple of days. It came on suddenly and he isn't getting better."

"Well, I am sure he is getting good care and they will soon find out what it is. The doctors and nurses there are quite good."

"I know. The nurses there are kind and look after him well, but I live in the country and I can't stay with him as long as I would like after I leave work."

"I think I can help," you answer. "I work at the hospital in the laboratory, and I will check on his condition and let you know. I will also take you back home after you visit with him. That way you can stay with him as long as you want."

"Would you do that for me? You don't even know me."

"Well can you think of a better way to get to know you? To get to know each other?"

" I agree with you," she says, obviously very relieved.

After you part you go to the children's ward and enquire about his condition. Fortunately, it is nothing really serious, just a slight viral infection. He is on the mend. The next day you are in your best friend's office across the street from the restaurant when you spot her having lunch. You hurry over, and surprise her when you address her by her surname, which she has not told you. She has only given you her christian name and details of her son's condition. It has been easy to go to the children's ward and get details from his chart. She is elated at the good news and you talk for a long time. You become good friends after that, and soon after, as the relationship grows, you get closer. You fall in love again.

Sarah is a good home-maker. She cooks and bakes well. She is a good mother, although she tends to spoil her son who is the center of her life. You have enjoyable times together going to plays and dances, going to the cricket club together and taking drives in the country or on the other side of the island to picnic on the beaches with the roaring surf of the rugged Atlantic side. You learn about her life during those times.

You learn later that she also has a daughter. She has never married. Not that it matters to you. Her son's father, whom she cared a lot about, had nearly been killed in a motorcycle accident, losing one of his feet at that time. Her daughter is living with her aunt in New York, but they are close and keep in constant contact. When you met she didn't have any serious romantic attachments, for which you are glad, for you are able to fill that void.

A short time after you become close you learn that her sister who is in Toronto has sponsored her and that she is due to leave to go 'up North'. Fate has intervened again in your life. You assist in all the preparations for her departure and drive her to the airport, and then she is gone.

She doesn't forget you though, and soon after you resume contact. She invites you to visit her. It is snowing lightly when she and her family meet you at the airport as the plane lands. You have come on a short vacation, but during that time it is idyllic in this new clean, progressive city, so different from that other North American country. You feel at home here. Her family makes you feel so welcome that you make the decision to emigrate there. You apply to one of the largest hospitals in the city for a job in the laboratory, and after the interview you are successful. You accept the job and return home at the end of that vacation and make your application for immigrant status to Canada. Approval of your immigration application comes shortly after and you make preparations to make your home 'up North' and begin a new journey in your life.

You ask her to marry you. She says yes.

Now, as the plane moves down the runway you look out your window as you did so many years before when you made your sojourn to the 'land of milk and honey', where the streets were 'paved with gold', fools' gold, with different feelings this time. You are embarking on a different adventure in a different country.

It is exciting starting over in this exciting new place. Your job provides the challenges and stimulation that you need and you soon take your place among the West Indian 'exile' community. You make new friends, go to home parties, and become part of the 'exile' community. You meet many friends from back home and that phase of your life begins to fade from your consciousness. Life is enjoyable.

Sarah fits into the life of a new immigrant easily. She is an easy learner, although she is not an ardent student of higher learning, preferring to attend to the duties of the home. She works in the stock market, entering into the work of data entry easily, and moves steadily upward in the organization. She has an easy-going manner, but is not afraid to let people who annoy her have a 'piece of her mind' when the occasion arises. She lets you know, in no uncertain terms, when she isn't pleased with things you do.

"I tell you to keep yuh belt in yuh hand," one of her brothers is always admonishing you when these times occur and arguments takw place between you. But confrontation and argument are not in your nature. Years later, in changed circumstances, you wonder if you should have heeded his advice.

The Meeting

"Fasten your seat belts, please, and bring your seats into the upright position."

The pleasant voice of the attractive blonde flight attendant intrudes on your thoughts. You look out of the window as the jet moves slowly down the taxi way. As she gives her instructions on the use of the life belt and the safety and emergency procedures, you glance around at your seat mate. You notice that your neighbor in the window seat, a pretty young lady, seems to be having trouble with her seat belt.

"Here, let me help you," you say, reaching across and straightening out the belt which has become caught under the arm rest of her seat. She seems tense, and a slight film of perspiration shines on her forehead.

"Thanks," she says quietly as you snap the buckle. Her voice seems strained.

"Is this the first time you are traveling?" you ask.

"Yes, I've never flown before."

"Well don't worry about it. I've flown many times, and I've lived to be able to tell you not to be afraid." You seek to reassure her.

"Thanks," she mumbles, but it is obvious that you have not succeeded in your attempt to comfort her. She still holds her body rigid and upright, and grips the armrest so tightly that the muscles on her forearm stand out prominently.

The plane turns at the end of the tarmac, and as the whine of the engines increase in pitch it begins to move faster along the runway. The nose lifts and as the angle increases it seems to leap into the air. You suddenly feel your arm gripped tightly. You look around to see your neighbor, eyes closed, breathing quickly and obviously very afraid. Your attempt at levity and reassurance has not calmed her.

"Don't worry," you say gently, "we are quite safe. Open your eyes. As you can see, we've left the ground. Look out the window."

She slowly opens her eyes, and as she realizes that the plane is indeed airborne, she exhales. The tenseness gradually leaves her body although she still holds your arm tightly, but as she relaxes she releases the grip, giving you a shy glance and smile, as she places hers on her lap.

"Sorry I gripped you so tightly," she says," but I was really afraid."

"It's all right, I understand. Everyone is afraid when they venture into the unknown for the first time or when they attempt something they have never done before."

The seat belt sign goes off, and as the cabin crew start their preparations to minister to the needs of the passengers, your attention is drawn to a slight sniffling from the window seat ahead of you. You see that it is occupied by an attractive, well-dressed young woman, who is making an effort to keep her tear-filled eyes dry with the tiny handkerchief in her hand.

Your seat mate reaches over the seat and touches her gently on her shoulder. The gesture is returned with a quick intertwining of fingers, and then she turns back to the window, looking down at the fast disappearing island. She looks back longingly, as if she wants to bring it with her. It is apparent from the brief gesture that there is a bond between the two of them, and that they are both moved by this departure from the island.

Passengers soon begin to move around as the drinks cart moves down the aisle. Your seat mate is completely relaxed by the time the attendant reaches your row of seats. She asks for a glass of orange juice, you order a rum and coke.

"What's your name?" you ask her, trying to strike up a conversation.

"Elaine," she answers. Her voice is mellow, smooth, and has a pleasant tone. It is a voice you want to hear more of.

"And where are you going to in Canada, Elaine?" You ask, wanting to hear her voice again.

"I'm going to Toronto," she answers.

"Are you going to join your family there?"

"No, I have no family there, not even friends. I expect to be working for a family in Forest Hills, although I have no idea where Forest Hills is, or what the family is like."

"Then how did you get the job?"

"I was recruited through the House Craft Center and the government. I am going on the Domestic Scheme*. My friend in front is going too."

"And what is your friend's name?"

"She's Mildred. She's going to work with a family somewhere on Avenue Road. This is all new to us. Neither one of us has left home before."

You are thoroughly intrigued. Here are two very attractive, sensitive daughters of the soil, going out to a strange new land, innocent to the world, unprotected and friendless, but willing to brave the unknown. What do they know of their employers, their likes and dislikes, their temperaments, their desires, their needs, or their wants? What is the driving force behind this desire to leave home and become exiles?

They know nothing, but like brides in some societies who are chosen, they are going, trusting, hoping, and praying for kindness. Wishing for happiness, wanting the things which would make them better off, which would make them independent.

They are going with only their abilities, their faith, the prayers of those they had left behind, and the burning desire to reach a goal with the self confidence of the exile.

As the two of you converse you realize that she seems

almost happy to be getting away from the island, but when she speaks of her small son and the need to leave him with her mother, you detect the sadness in her heart. She speaks freely and naturally, intelligently, and seems anxious to keep the conversation going. She is also funny, making you laugh often with clever anecdotes.

Mildred is soon pulled into the conversation. She too is anxious for friendly company. This keeps the loneliness away for a while. Elaine has a refreshing sense of humor, and keeps you regaled with stories about people in her village. Mildred leans over the seat to join in the conversation. You soon become friends. You are no different from them, for you too are going to Canada for the first time. You are going into exile again.

In between lapses in the conversation when they are looking out of the windows at islands the plane is passing over, you have the opportunity to observe them. They were both beautiful.

Elaine reminds you of Nefertiti, queen of the Nile. There is regal beauty and bearing in the way she carries herself. Mildred's beauty is different. Hers belongs on the covers of fashion magazines. It is the kind which would cause photographers to fight with each other to get her in range of their lenses. And when she leaves her seat to walk down the aisle, you see how shapely she is, how upright is her bearing, which causes her breasts to jut out, and how easy is the swing of her legs.

Time passes quickly, and the sound of the engines combined with the afternoon meal and drinks pushes you into the arms of Morpheus before you are aware of it. You begin to doze off, comparing her walk to something you had learned in Physics, and you fall asleep remembering the formula for the laws of simple harmonic motion—the swing of the pendulum. That's what her walk and the consequent motion of the two halves of her round bottom are like. It is the easy motion of the pendulum swinging the same distance each side. The motion is exquisite: tick, tock, tick, tock, from side to side, right, left, right.....

The sound of the seat belt sign coming on awakens you, and the announcement that the plane is preparing to land at Toronto seems to catch most people by surprise. Time has passed quickly, and everyone begins to make preparations for the landing. You exchange addresses and phone numbers with Elaine and Mildred, promising to keep in contact with them. Elaine has no trouble with her seat-belt this time, but as the plane descends she reaches out for your hand. This time your fingers lock, but she keeps her eyes closed and gasps audibly as the bump of the wheels on the ground indicates that the plane has landed.

The passage through immigration and customs after a seemingly interminable walk through the long tunnels is relatively swift. You meet again outside.

Mildred meets her new employers. They are Jewish. They arrive in a Rolls Royce. She waves to you through the back window, but there seems to be apprehension in her expression rather than excitement. Elaine soon leaves in a Lincoln for Forest Hills. She is chauffeur-driven. You and your wife-to-be, who meets you as you come outside, leave by airport limousine for St. Clair Avenue. It is not far from Avenue Road or Forest Hills. Like them, you are starting over, trusting in the future, and trusting in yourself and your abilities. You are rejoining the army of immigrants leaving the island for overseas adventures.

You are all destined to meet again, and you do many times, and they continue their narratives, and you learn about their lives and what drives them, their hopes, fears, ambitions, and all aspects of their relationships. And you become friends, and hear their life stories.

PART V

Exile

Mildred

Mildred was glad that she lived so high in Bathurst Street, almost at Steeles, the end of the bus run. The family with whom she was working had moved since she had first begun to work in their house. Bathurst near Steeles was a rural area, once all farmland, which was quickly becoming populated. Apartment buildings were springing up, seemingly overnight, and businesses were beginning to move into the area bringing more people and shops. Many people did not get on at this stop, and it meant that she had her choice of seats. She liked to sit at the window which gave her a view of all the expensive houses she passed on her way down to Bloor Street. She liked the few moments of solitude she could enjoy until it got further down when it became crowded. From the window she could also see Elaine when she boarded and could often have space for her on the seat. She looked forward to these Thursday meetings with her friend and compatriot, when they could talk about home and friends and reminisce.

She and Elaine had become friends when they met at the Housecraft Centre, where they learned to become 'good domestics', which would give them the chance to emigrate to this country of cold and snow and ice and loneliness, but also of opportunity.

Many times since her arrival she had cried herself to sleep thinking about home, thinking about her changed circumstances, thinking about her family and wondering if she had made the right choice.

It was only because of Elaine that she was able to persevere, for Elaine always comforted her with the admonition to 'keep your eyes on your goal'—the goal of landed-immigrant status—and bear all the indignities you have to bear until you reach that goal. When she wavered, lying in her cold room in the attic of the home of her wealthy but stingy employers, she often reminded herself that even though she was a domestic, she was not a domestic in her mind. She often remembered Vi and understood what Vi had to go through and admired her, because Vi always bore her status with dignity. She resolved to bear hers with stoicism and that same dignity, firmly believing that that was not her destiny, but a temporary stop on her highway of life.

She saw Elaine getting on and was glad that no one was sitting next to her. She made room for her, taking her bag out of the seat, which was her way of reserving it, for she knew that the white people who got on the bus would be reluctant to sit next to her in any case, but she still used her bag to further secure the space. When the white people got on the bus they usually looked at her for a fleeting moment and then quickly looked away, for she had gotten into the habit of looking them straight in their eyes and they soon shifted their glances.

Elaine came hurrying down the aisle and plopped down in the seat.

"Girlfriend, I am so glad to see you," she said, "That mistress of mine didn't want me to come downtown today, saying she had to go out, and wanted me to babysit her 'precious' cat. I had to remind her that today was my day off, and by law I was entitled to it, and I had made a business arrangement that I had to keep. and in any case the cat didn't need any baby-sitting."

"I'm glad you came," Mildred answered, "for I really need your company today. I have been thinking about home all night and I just had to get out of the house. This domestic thing is getting to me."

"That's funny, I was thinking about home too. I miss my son

and it is only because I have you, Peter and the other girls that I am able to keep my sanity. I miss seeing black faces, for that area where I am working has only one black face in the entire district, and that is mine. The way some of them get on you would think they never even see a picture of a black person. Anyhow we have to hold on, we only have a short time to go now, and then it will be all over."

Elaine reached over and took Mildred's hand in hers.

"Don't worry, it will be alright. I am here for you, remember, we are friends." Mildred was close to tears, but the reassuring smile of her friend gave her comfort. As the bus continued down towards Bloor Street she became immersed in her thoughts and memories.

The crowded bus was taking a long time to reach the Bathurst and Bloor Station, the meeting place for all those who had come to this country as immigrants, male and female, West Indian and European, and who made Toronto their home. But it was a special place for Barbadians, especially those females who had come as domestics.

With each stop the bus made on its long journey from the suburbs down to the city, her frustration increased. She looked forward to this weekly ritual, this coming together of kindred spirits, this meeting of souls. They had lots in common.

All during the week the anticipation of this event helped her maintain her sanity. It helped her endure the indignities she had to undergo with her employers. It helped her maintain her focus and keep her objective in proper perspective. She knew what she wanted, where she wanted to go, and how to get there. But unless she had these weekly meetings, she felt that she would lose this perspective.

It was difficult without the comradeship and support of the others. She needed them and they needed her. They were all the same. They had the same feelings; the feelings of exiles.

As the bus came down the long road her mind drifted back to home. She had been a Queen's College girl. Queen's College was the top girls' secondary school on the island. Back home she was considered as upper middle-class and she was proud of it.

She had lived in a large upstairs house in Bank Hall which was near enough to Strathclyde, where some of the white people of the island lived to be considered semi-exclusive.

At one time Black people from Bank Hall, like all other Black people, couldn't live in Strathclyde. Only white people lived there. If Black people had to pass through that short avenue, they had to pass on the Peterkin's Land side of the rails which ran down the center of the road dividing it into Strathclyde on one side, and Peterkin's Land on the other.

Strathclyde was exclusive. Peterkin's Land was not. Black people crossed from Peterkin's land to Strathclyde to work as domestic servants. The railings down the centre of the road divided them.

Bank Hall was close enough. It was semi-exclusive. As a result the residents lived accordingly, they lived as if they were not there; as if they did not exist, as if it was a favor to live close to Strathclyde. They lived quietly, very quietly.

Her father was a senior civil servant, almost a permanent secretary. Her mother didn't work. It wouldn't have been proper. She stayed at home to look after Mildred and her younger brother, who was a student at Combermere. Combermere was below Harrison College and Queen's College in status.

At Combermere there were no sixth forms. You couldn't learn the sciences. You couldn't win a Barbados scholarship from Combermere. Combermere was semi-exclusive. Its brightest students had to leave and go to Harrison College if they could get in, and if they hoped to go further in their studies.

Mildred never had to provide for herself. Vi, the maid, adored her and looked after her every need. That didn't mean that she didn't or couldn't do house work. Her mother insisted that she keep her room neat and tidy at all times, that she learned to wash, sew, and even cook, and enforced her wishes with the strap. She was gentle though, and hardly ever raised her voice. She was quiet, almost to the point of being mistaken for being weak.

Mildred never liked peeling potatoes and onions and washing dishes though. She felt that these activities would destroy her lovely fingernails, which she kept well-manicured. She always took good care of her appearance, and was very careful to dress stylishly and well. She was proud without being vain.

Each Sunday the family went to the All Saint's Church as a unit. After the service, when they returned home, Vi would have a large meal on the table, and everyone would sit and bow their heads. Prayers would be said by a different member of the family every time, and at the end of the meal they would retire to their rooms for Sunday rest.

It was a peaceful home. It was a nice atmosphere in which the children grew. A harsh word never passed between father and mother in the presence of the children. They were nice people—the white folks in Strathclyde said so, behind the walls of their homes, in their 'drawing rooms'.

Mildred had reached as far as she could go educationally in the island. She had obtained her Advanced Level certificates and was considered 'bright'. She was not scholarship material, though.

Since leaving school she couldn't find a job. Even though her father tried to get her into the civil service, he was unsuccessful. She tried for months. She wrote countless letters of application to countless places. She tried everything; notices in the newspapers, friends, family, employment agencies, even strangers. Once when she was at a party she was introduced to a politician who promised to 'pull a few strings' and get her something when she mentioned how difficult it was to find work.

She believed him. He seemed so sincere and honest. He was

a Minister in Government.

She was surprised late one evening when the telephone rang, and she heard his voice at the other end. When he invited her out to dinner to 'discuss her resume', among other things, she jumped at the opportunity. She was glad for the chance to get out of the house, for she had become bored, discouraged, and even slightly depressed at her inactivity, socially and otherwise. She looked forward to the meeting, and as she chose her clothes carefully, she thought fleetingly that it might be interesting to flirt a little with him. She chose an off-the-shoulder white sleeveless dress which hugged her waist and showed off her shape to perfection. She had a very nice figure.

She had no romantic involvement. In fact, she had never had any. A slight case of puppy love for one of her teachers hardly qualified as romantic involvement. Besides, her prospective date was good-looking, and appeared very distinguished in his high collar Shirt-Jac*. Maybe she might even come to like him, she fantasized. But then she put these thoughts from her head with the self-admonition that this was going to be strictly a business dinner.

When she told her parents of her dinner appointment with Michael, she was surprised at her father's reaction. It was as if he really did not want her to go, but yet was afraid to say so.

"How did you meet him?" he asked.

"Oh, we were introduced at Sandra's party two weeks ago."

"But how did he get your phone number?"

"He asked me for it and I gave it to him. I didn't see anything wrong in doing that."

"You know he is a very important person in the government. He is a Minister."

"So what? He is just another man as far as I am concerned." Mildred answered sharply. She could feel her anger rising.

"Well if you are going out to dinner, I hope you will conduct yourself in the proper manner. Don't do anything to embarrass him."

Mildred was angry now and hardly realized what she was saying before the words came out.

"Father," she only called him 'father' when she was angry, "I am your daughter, my behavior will be the product of your teaching. I find you very insensitive to be concerned only with if I embarrass him. Is there a possibility that he will embarrass me? Don't you trust me?"

"He will never embarrass you. He is a minister of government, he knows how to conduct himself properly." Her father answered defensively.

"He is a man. He is human. Even ministers of government are human."

For the first time in her life Mildred raised her voice at her father. The tears came flowing and she turned and ran upstairs to her bedroom. She flung herself on the bed and sobbed uncontrollably. Her father had hurt her with his words and attitude more than she had been hurt before.

A short time later her mother came into the room, sat next to her on the bed, and, gently placing her hand on Mildred's shoulder, tried to comfort her.

"Don't be angry with your father my dear," she said softly, "he didn't mean to hurt you."

"But why did he seem to care so little about me then? He seemed to be only interested in Michael."

Her mother was conciliatory.

"You must understand. He is a civil servant. He can't get it out of his system. It is part of him. It's all he knows. He has been in the system too long, and he is loyal to his employers, the political bosses."

"But surely he can't be so weak." Mildred said looking intently at her mother, "we are only going to dinner."

"I know dear, but I think that deep down he is afraid for you and wants to protect you."

"Protect me from what?" Mildred asked, seeking an answer in her mother's eyes.

"I think he loves you so much, that he doesn't want to say what he is afraid of. Maybe you will know and understand later what he is really afraid of. Now dry your tears and come downstairs."

And with this she kissed Mildred gently on her forehead and went downstairs. For a long time afterward, Mildred lay in her bed thinking of her mother's words and trying to understand the meaning of what she had said.

When she came downstairs her father was nowhere around. She found this very strange, because he never missed the evening news on the television. He was always there.

Seeing the wondering looks, her mother just said quietly:

"He has gone walking." Mildred understood that her mother considered the matter closed.

Promptly at seven-thirty that Saturday evening, the knock at the door indicated that Michael had arrived.

When she came downstairs her father had already opened the door and invited him in. Somehow she felt a tinge of annoyance at her father's attitude. Even here in his own home, the obsequiousness of the civil servant was evident. His deference to the minister, his seeming inability to see himself as equal when away from the office, upset her. Was this the result of indoctrination? Was it fear of victimization? Was it the result of years of belief in the superiority of the politician even though they had to be taught everything, had to be spoon-fed and protected when they had won their seat to Parliament? Or was this subservient attitude due to a desire to maintain his status and 'security'?

The feeling left her quickly when she greeted her escort. He smiled as he put his hand lightly on her shoulder, and guided her through the door.

"Don't worry, Mr. Marshall," he said turning slightly to her father. "I'll take good care of her and bring her back safely, and early."

"I'm sure you will Mr. Minister," her father answered. He

kept both hands behind his back, and bowed slightly. "I trust you."

Mildred felt that feeling of annoyance creep up again. What about her? Didn't he trust her? Did he trust the minister only because he was a minister? Did he only believe him because he was a politician? What happened to people when they became civil servants? What happened to their humanness? What happened to their independence?

She was so preoccupied with her thoughts that she reacted with a start when Michael touched her lightly on her elbow as he opened the front door of the car for her. She looked back and saw her father framed in the doorway. And she caught a fleeting glimpse of what seemed to her to be his shoulders drooping ever so slightly. He seemed a little older at that moment.

She realized that Michael was talking to her and that the car was moving.

"Do you know where I am taking you tonight?" he asked.

"No, I felt that I should leave the choice to you."

"Well I'm taking you to The Castle, Sam Lord's Castle. I made reservations for us."

"I'm really impressed," she answered, genuinely pleased. She had never been to The Castle before, and was thrilled at the thought of being taken to such an elegant and expensive place. She felt special, but her consciousness was stimulated. She had often thought about what was happening in the country and to the country. Wasn't it funny, she thought, since the famous building had been purchased by an international hotel chain, it had been turned into a hotel where the local people had great difficulty gaining entrance.

Formerly, on Sunday afternoons, citizens could walk in through the gates and walk freely through the grounds, admiring the well manicured lawns and the trim hedges. One could take pictures with the famous building and the fountains as a background. There was no difficulty in walking down the steep steps in the cliff to get to the wide beach which sloped to the emerald water which came rushing in over the reefs to wash sea grapes on the sand. And at night, when the moon shone silver on the sea, one could imagine the sailors on the ships out at sea, fooled by the lanterns placed in the trees, crashing to their doom on the reefs while Sam Lord and his cohorts plundered them and returned to shore with their booty.

But all that was changed now. You had to be 'somebody', or with 'somebody', to get in. There was a guard at the gate, and a chain, and any and everybody couldn't get in. The Castle was exclusive. Everything was changing. Everywhere was changing. Everybody was changing.

This place should have been a national treasure; a place where the inhabitants could feel at one with their history. It should have been a place where everybody could be a part of their past. Now that was taken away forever, and generations would be born, they would die, and never be part of themselves. They would never be a part of or see their history. They would never feel a oneness with their country. They would always be outside the chain, on the Peterkin's Land side. Always on the Peterkin's Land side. And this was happening all over the island.

Where one formerly had free access to the sea on the south and west coasts, hotels and expensive houses were springing up. One couldn't even see the beaches from the road. Even where the roads passed along the seaside and had been there for generations, they were shifted inland so that the occupants of the buildings would have exclusive access to the sea. They wouldn't have to cross the road. They could sit on their balconies and sip their drinks, and gaze over the calm waters. The locals wouldn't even be able to see the sea.

They would have to pass through narrow paths in the woods, and between buildings away from the sea, on the Peterkin's Land side. Always on the Peterkin's Land side.

Her thoughts turned back to the present.

It was a pleasant drive through the countryside. The wind was cool and the moonlight, broken occasionally by the sugar cane stalks which grew on both sides of the road, gave softness to the night. The sound of the tires on the black tarmac sang a soothing lullaby which relaxed her to the point where she shifted in her seat so that she was almost laying back. Michael looked at her and smiled.

"Comfortable?" he asked.

"Oh yes, it's such a beautiful night. I wish it could be like this forever." She answered. They lapsed back into silence, occupied with their own thoughts.

After a while they reached the columned entrance to The Castle. The gate attendant recognized the car and its driver and directed them in with a wave of his hand. They stopped a few yards from the entrance steps. He got out, opened the door for her, and escorted her up the broad steps into the lobby.

Mildred drew in her breath at the magnificence before her; the large chandeliers, the massive paintings of former colonial overlords, the dark mahogany furniture which reflected their age, and the shining parquet floor with its expensive carpets. As they walked through the lobby and onto the balcony overlooking the lawns and fountain, brightly lit in the moonlight, she felt a sudden rush of warmth and moisture in her loins, and a stiffening of her nipples. She was sexually aroused by the sheer beauty around her, and the romantic atmosphere it all created. Her escort came behind her, rested his hands lightly on her shoulders, and pulled her gently toward him. She leaned back and felt the warmth of his body. The moisture came again. This was a new experience for her.

A waiter appeared out of nowhere with a tray and glasses of champagne. They each took one, and her escort lifted his in a toast.

"To an enjoyable evening and all that follows," he said gently.

"Thanks for your attention," she smiled as she clinked his glass with hers and raised it to her lips.

Soon after, the waiter ushered them to their seats in a small alcove in the dining room. This ensured complete privacy, away from any prying eyes. Momentarily, Mildred was apprehensive. Why this secrecy to enjoy a business dinner, she wondered. She looked at him and saw briefly in his eyes a look which sent a tremor through her. She couldn't put her finger on it or describe it, but it was not the look she felt should be there at this time, in such a romantic setting.

He must have read her thoughts.

"Are you worried because we are so private?" He asked. His voice was almost seductive in its tone.

"No, not really. I'm not worried."

"Don't bother yourself my dear. A person in my position must be careful when we are out in public. The press is always looking for ways to embarrass us, although I am used to them. It's you I want to protect."

"Thank you very much," she said, genuinely pleased, "that's very thoughtful of you."

Somehow his words still seemed hollow, and she couldn't silence the tiny alarm bells which seemed to be ringing—those bells which seemed intent on changing the atmosphere of what was a lovely evening so far.

As the waitress brought their courses, conversation between them slowed. She had begun to enjoy her meal at first, but as the dishes from the main course—lobster vinaigrette with a butter sauce, rice pilaf, gungo peas, mini corn and carrots accompanied by a bottle of excellent chardonnay—were being moved away, she became more apprehensive.

Michael hadn't said one word about her resume or anything remotely connected with a job. Should she open the subject? Should she wait for him to begin the discussion? But why wouldn't he say anything about it? All he was doing was making small talk, complementing her on her dress, her earrings, her shoes, staring pointedly at her breasts, and smiling wickedly around the rim of the wine glass he put to his lips. She couldn't bear it any longer and broached the subject.

"Michael," she said softly, "it was lovely to be invited to dinner, but you said that you wanted to discuss my resume, and, I assume, the possibility of getting a job."

"That's true, my dear, but the night is yet young, and I didn't want to spoil the romanticism of this wonderful moonlit night by discussing such mundane things. We'll have lots of time for that subject later."

She felt helpless. He was right. The atmosphere was not conducive to that subject. She decided to relax and enjoy the balance of the evening. The music of the small combo enhanced the mood.

After the coffee cups had been removed, he got up from the table, came around to her side, and gently lifted her from her chair.

"Let's take a walk outside and enjoy the beauty of the Castle. The gardens are beautiful and with the lights they are really lovely."

"Alright," she said, and got up.

With his arms resting lightly around her waist, he escorted her out on to the balcony, down the steep steps, and onto the lush dew-wet grass. The droplets of water from the fountain created myriad rainbows in the flood lights shining from the ground. Scarcely feeling the ground beneath her feet, she found herself on the beach behind the castle.

The waves were pounding over the reefs and rushing to the shore to throw themselves helplessly on the sand as if they were trying to reach somewhere, but just not getting there, and sliding back, to come rushing up again, just falling short of their objective. For many, life is like the surf, always falling just short of the objective.

Michael stopped her gently, bent down, and removed her high heeled shoes.

"You can't really walk comfortably on the sand in these."

"That's true," she said softly.

She didn't recognize her own voice, and this scared her. What's happening to me? She thought. I feel all soft inside. Why this constant moisture between my legs?

They walked arm in arm until they had gone far down the beach, and the music from the band playing for the dancers at the castle was almost a whisper. There was a steady refreshing breeze blowing, making the casuarinas sigh as it passed through their branches.

Without being aware of what was happening, she felt her head being tilted, and lips resting softly on hers. A thrill ran through her, starting with a tingle at the top of her head, and coursing through her body with such intensity that she felt her toes curling in the sand, feeling every tiny grain on the soles of her feet. It seemed that each one touched a nerve.

She involuntarily opened her mouth and felt his tongue enter. Hers met his and intertwined with it. She sucked on his lips and pulled him to her, thrusting her pelvis against his hardness. For what seemed an eternity to her, they remained locked in that embrace. The moisture was more obvious.

He soon broke the kiss, and with a gasp she realized that he had freed her breasts from the confines of the low cut dress. She wore no brassieres. Her young breasts were upright and prominent, and the small nipples now enlarged and projecting. Around each one it seemed as if the pores themselves were projecting in the intensity of her sexuality. Michael's lips settled on a nipple, and as he sucked on it she felt as if her head would burst. She pulled him harder to her chest, as if she wanted him inside her. She was gasping and moaning, but she thought it was the wind blowing through the casuarinas. Surely those sounds couldn't be coming from her.

When he finally pulled his head away, she thought she still felt his lips on her breast, and the sensation of his suction remained. When he lowered her to the sand, with her head resting on the sea-grape vines, she was hardly aware of it. She only knew that she was on a cloud, floating, floating, and never wanting to come to earth. She was completely relaxed, and every part of her body felt as if it were made of cotton, like the pods of wild cotton growing beside the road, taken by a puff of wind and floating in on the currents of air.

It felt perfectly natural to raise and open her legs when she lay down, and when he kissed her navel, the sensation made her gasp again. His tongue started flames throughout her body, and when he moved her white french-cut panties aside and kissed her pubis, she felt a muscle-tightening orgasm begin from her feet to reach her brain. She almost fainted. And the moisture came.

And the more he sucked the more she wanted. She never wanted it to stop. Her cries were unintelligible. She was crying, moaning, and talking all at the same time.

Another orgasm tortured her.

There was a brief, unwanted respite when he removed his pants. She instinctively opened her legs wider. She felt his penis at the entrance, and, locking her legs around his buttock, pulled him into her. She was a virgin. There was no pain. A moment of discomfort, but he was inside easily. It was the moisture. Even as he was thrusting, new sensations were coursing through her body. Her arms circled his muscular body and pulled him closer. Her hips moved in a rhythm which was out of Africa.

She felt the orgasm starting again. Her movements became more violent, and she developed a strength she never knew she had. Even though Michael was so much heavier, she was lifting him with each upward thrust of her body. She wanted more of him inside. And it came. A gut-wrenching, eye-turning, mouth-screaming, muscle-tensing orgasm. She fainted.

The coolness of the water on her cheek revived her. She opened her eyes to find Michael pouring sea water from his cupped hands onto her forehead.

"What happened?" She asked, looking around. She was sitting on the sand but she couldn't recognize the area. The sand around looked as if a herd of animals had passed through. The sea grape vines were torn from their bed on the sand, and her dress was all stained with their juices.

He didn't answer. He just squatted in front of her with his hands outstretched, the sea-water dripping through his fingers. He just squatted looking at her.

She couldn't understand the look on his face, which was fully revealed by the bright moonlight, previously blotted out by the clouds overhead. Now that the clouds were past, it became one of those moonlit nights which can only be seen on a tropic island. One of those nights when it is almost as clear as day, but with softness which, together with that breeze from the ocean and the rustling of the trees, creates an ambiance which cannot be duplicated anywhere else.

Michael's eyes probed into her steadily, questioningly, and still he didn't say anything. She couldn't understand. He seemed almost angry. But why was he angry? What was it all about?

"Michael," she said questioningly, "why are you looking at me like that. What happened?"

"Where did you learn to screw like that?" He asked.

"What do you mean, I don't understand." She was really perplexed now.

"You went completely wild, I couldn't control you." He answered, his voice rising. "And your movements, I've never had anybody like you before."

"You are the first man I've ever had intercourse with," she answered, and at the realization of what had taken place, her face became suffused and shame flooded her.

"Suppose someone had heard you?" Michael got up from his squatting position and moved a little away from her. "If somebody had heard you, they would surely have thought that I was taking advantage of you."

"But didn't you?" She answered.

"I most certainly did not," he replied indignantly, "you were in for it from the beginning. When I pushed my finger inside you, you were all wet, and when I kissed you, you kissed me back as if it were something you were accustomed doing."

That made her angry.

"You are the first man I ever really kissed or had sex with. I don't know what went on. I don't remember anything from the time you kissed me until now. So don't make those insinuations."

"Well you certainly didn't wuk-up as if I was the first." Michael was furious now. "And why did you have to faint? Suppose somebody had seen you like that? I have a position to protect."

Mildred couldn't believe her ears.

"You are the most selfish, insensitive person I have ever met. All you are thinking about is your position. What about me? Don't you care about my feelings? We were supposed to have dinner and talk about a job. You played with my emotions and my sensitivities, and now you are talking about your position?" She was shouting.

He looked around to see if anyone was within earshot. He reached out to touch her.

"Come now, you don't have to shout," he said trying to calm her.

"Who the hell do you think you are?" she shouted, her breast rising and falling with the intensity of her anger. "Who de shite gives you the God-dammed right to play with my emotions like that? I have feelings!"

He came nearer to her. He was now really alarmed. He had never before met such anger in a woman. He didn't know how to handle it. This woman was different. Her reactions were different. His other women never reacted in this way. They were almost afraid of his importance, and treated him with deference.

"Don't you come near to me! You hear!" she screamed at him. Michael was in shock. He was not accustomed to being spoken to like this, especially not by a woman. He stopped with his hand still reaching for her.

"Get away from me," she said as she jumped toward him, and with a mighty shove dumped him right in the path of a large incoming wave.

He got the full force of it and before he realized what was happening, he was rolling in the water. The wave held him. It wouldn't let him go. It almost drowned him in its anger. He was completely soaked and out of breath when it finally threw him on the sand, and he regained his feet.

That sound. Did he hear the wind whispering to the trees? Was it listening to them?

Mildred had begun walking briskly in the direction from which they had come. By the time he caught up with her, she was climbing the steps cut out of the cliff face which led up to the castle. Without looking left or right, she walked straight through the lobby, shoes in hand, rumpled, leaf-stained dress and all, down the steps, and stood waiting by the front door of his car. Her chest was heaving with the intensity of her anger, and her blazing eyes matched the set of her mouth. She stood, arms akimbo, tapping her bare feet as she waited for him.

Michael followed leaving a trail of water behind his footsteps, which in turn left sand and water stains on the carpet with each step. The waiters and guests looked at him, and then at each other, and then at him—head bent, trying to hurry in a dignified manner, but looking completely undignified.

By morning everybody would know. He was sure of it. He silently opened the car door for her, went around to his side, and got in. Water drained from all parts of his suit, and when he sat the entire seat quickly became stained.

He clenched his fist in anger. He always kept his car immaculate. He usually spent hours washing and cleaning every part of it, even taking off the wheels to scrub under the fenders. If the rain fell he left it in the garage at home, and took a taxi wherever he had to go. Now the seats were stained, water and sand was all over the carpet, and he knew how wet carpet smelled after a few days. The thought made him angrier.

He started the car and drove off. He was sure that shortly after he passed back through the entrance, he heard the gatekeeper laughing loudly. He was sure of it.

He imagined how his other cabinet colleagues would laugh. Although they pretended to respect him, he knew they didn't like him very much. They were all hypocrites.

Neither of them spoke on the drive back to her home. Shortly before they reached her home, however, he turned to her, anger in his voice.

"How could you go and faint? How could you do that to me? How could you push me in the water? Look at my clothes, look at my car. I'll be the laughing stock of the island." His voice was almost hysterical. He was uncomfortable in his wet suit and shoes. Whenever he shifted in the seat, water drained into the growing puddle on the carpet.

Mildred didn't say a word, but there was tightness to her lips and she stared unblinking ahead.

They reached her home, and without waiting for him, she opened the door as the car came to a halt. She turned to him and, raising her hand, slapped him in his face. The force of the blow left the imprint of her fingers on his cheek.

"I fainted because I have feelings!" She answered icily. "You will never understand, and you can kiss my ass. I don't ever want to see you again, and don't call me either."

She got out of the car and, ascending the steps quickly, opened the door and went directly to her room. She did not look back. She didn't see her father standing in the darkness of the living room, neither did she know how long he stood there looking up the stairs after she had passed, nor did she see the look of resignation in his eyes.

He understood. Things would never be the same again.

Michael drove away quickly, the tyres of his powerful car screeching as he stepped on the accelerator. The evening had been a disaster.

The sun was streaming through the curtain when Mildred, awakened by the knock at her door, opened her eyes. With a start, she realized that she was completely naked. The memory of the night's events flashed before her mind's eye in a split second, and she remembered the haste with which she had torn off her dress and panties and showered, rubbing her skin vigorously as if she wanted to scrub away the events of the night, and flinging herself on the bed, sobbing into her pillow until sleep had taken over.

The knocking came again and her mother called softly,

"Mildred, are you awake? Can I come in?"

"Yes, come in." Mildred answered as she found her robe and put it on. Her mother entered with a tray of orange juice, tea and toast, and a boiled egg.

"You came in late last night so I knew you would miss breakfast. I made some for you." She placed the tray on the dressing table and came over. She looked at Mildred and, reaching out, gathered her into her arms and held her tightly.

Tears started in Mildred's eyes and fell on to her mother's shoulder.

"You don't have to say anything my dear. I know. I understand. Don't worry, I am here for you and I will always be by your side."

Mildred felt her mother's love flowing from body to body.

"Mom, I'm sorry. I know Dad is going to be angry, but I have to tell you what happened so that you will understand."

"I know my dear. Eat your breakfast and shower, and then you can come downstairs and we will talk."

She kissed Mildred lightly on her cheek and left the room, softly closing the door behind her. Mildred remained in the same spot for some time, looking at the door. Her mother knew. She was sure of it. She knew and understood, and still loved her.

Later that day she was sitting on the settee in the living room reading when her father entered. It was twilight. One of those cool Caribbean evenings just after the setting of the sun which had painted the cloud spattered sky with streaks of red and pink, when the breeze is a mere whisper, and the air is still in anticipation of the night. She looked up, and from the set of his lips, knew that he was angry. He came across the room and stood a few feet away from her.

"How could you?"

"How could I what, Dad?"

"Before you went to dinner last night, I distinctly remember speaking to you about embarrassing the Minister."

"Yes I remember," she answered guardedly.

"And yet you embarrassed him."

"Can I ask what you have heard to make you come to that conclusion?" Her voice was calm and controlled. After speaking with her mother earlier in the day and explaining the entire episode, Mildred knew that her mother was on her side.

"It is all over the place, even in one of the gossip columns of the newspaper."

"And exactly what has been printed?"

"It is said that he went to dinner and ended up having to drive home soaked to the skin, after being pushed in the water. He is so embarrassed he didn't even come to work today. I know you are the one the papers are talking about. I saw you when you came home last night."

"Well, father, I don't have to deny anything. We went out to dinner. We were supposed to discuss my resume and the possibility of getting a job. We didn't. Instead we went for a walk on the beach. We made love, and because of his insensitivity to my emotion and passion, I pushed him in the water. I am not sorry for what I did. I don't apologize for it, and on reflection I am glad I did it, and would do it again. People like him need to be put in their place."

He was perplexed by her attitude. How could she be so detached? For the first time he realized how mature she was. She had grown up before him. He still saw her as his little girl, but here she was calmly admitting that she had sex with a mature man, and seemed to be very matter of fact about it. His anger was replaced by confusion.

"How am I going to face him when he returns to work? I am sure to be transferred. These men can't take blows to their egos. I still have a long way to go until retirement. I have to think of my pension."

"Father," she said very quietly, almost patiently, "you have always been a good civil servant. You have experience and a good reputation. You don't have to be afraid of people like him. Make them respect you. What went on is between me and Michael. You can't be punished for my transgressions. Stand up for your rights, and don't be pushed around by anyone, least of all a politician."

"But you don't understand, this is the civil service. We have to work with them."

His excuse sounded feeble, and he realized that she was right. He looked at her fixedly for a long time. He was seeing a new woman. An independent woman. He turned and left the room.

Mildred remained seated in the night-darkened room long after he had gone, recalling the events which had led up to this confrontation with her father. Things would never be the same again between them.

By the next month Mildred knew that she was pregnant. She thought long and hard over what she would do. Abortion. There was no alternative.

She discussed it at length with her mother, who was pragmatic, and concurred. They both agreed that her father would never know about it. His Christian and obstinate views would never condone it, but Christianity couldn't be allowed to stand in the way of pragmatism and reality. Besides, he didn't have to know. It would be their secret; a secret between two women. Men didn't have to know everything.

It was painful and traumatic, and the sound of the suction apparatus as the fetus traveled through the tube and into the jar at the end had a more traumatic effect on her than she had thought it would. Her mother held her hand throughout the ordeal, firmly insisting to the doctor that she intended to be with her in the surgery, and cradled her in her arm all the way back home.

Wordlessly she lay beside Mildred on her bed, cradling her head until she fell asleep, and staying next to her for a long time after the moon had risen. The bond between them became stronger.

After that they spent many long hours talking about all sorts of things, life in general, men, love, and her future. Out of these discussions came the conclusion that she should go to the House Craft Center. Young ladies were being trained in home economics in preparation for emigration to Canada, as housemaids—domestics. Teachers and high school girls were the ones being recruited—good girls.

Mildred went, and it was there that she met Elaine. They became close friends. Elaine was always jovial, and her effervescent attitude was just what Mildred needed at this time. They discussed many things together, and realized that they had some things in common—a man had used them.

When she told her father about her plans for emigrating to Canada it caused another argument between them. Her mother supported her against him. He was very angry. As he said, 'his daughter was a Queen's College girl. How could she want to work as a housemaid in white people house, cleaning their toilets, and wiping up their mess?' He could never accept that. Even though she was from Bank Hall, she was from the Peterkin's Land side.

After this argument he didn't speak to her for a long time. He became very withdrawn, and there always seemed to be tension in the house. She told Vi what had happened and why she was leaving. Vi was so angry at what had taken place that she was ready to go and confront Michael right in his office. Vi didn't care what might happen to her, she would give her life for Mildred. Vi was from Peterkin's Land—but common sense prevailed and she soon settled down to the reality of Mildred's impending departure. As the time drew nearer she catered to Mildred's every whim, hugging her at every chance, and singing hymns all day as she did her housework. Occasionally Mildred would see her wiping a tear from her eyes, and those moments saddened her. Vi really loved her as if she were her own child.

As the time for her departure came closer her father became more morose and seemed to age visibly before them.

The night before she left, for the first time in her life, she heard her parents arguing loudly.

"I didn't raise my daughter and send her to Queen's College to clean out somebody's toilet. I couldn't live with that!" He shouted at her mother.

And her mother answering, her voice—that usually quiet, controlled, gentle voice—rising in anger.

"It is her life. She has made that decision, and you have to accept that. This place has no future, nothing to offer her. At least in Canada she will have a chance to better herself. There is no shame in doing an honest day's work, whatever it is, and it won't be forever. She has to go, she has to escape the quagmire that is this society, a society of hypocrites and charlatans, this dishonest society, this society of prejudice and discrimination. You have to open your eyes, you have to let go."

"I cannot, and will not accept that. She will be a servant." His voice was almost hysterical in its timbre. His eyes were staring and he was trembling violently. "She is a Queen's College girl. Don't you understand what that means in this country?" Tears filled his eyes.

Mildred, who observed all this from the top of the stairs,

was also in tears. She understood her father's pain. She was from the Peterkin's Land side, but she had crossed the barrier to Strathclyde. Strathclyde girls went to Queen's College.

He didn't come to the airport to see her off. That hurt her, but her mother softened the pain, assuring her that:

"He still loves you, but his pride is greater than his common sense, and he would prefer to shed his tears at home rather than at the airport."

He however sent a letter with a portion of money enclosed. Despite their differences of opinion he still loved her. She was the embodiment of his pride.

Her mother hugged her tightly, tears coursing down her cheek. Vi placed a small gold cross around her neck.

"God will guide you," she said softly as she kissed her. Mildred turned and walked quickly to the plane.

Although tears were close to spilling over she was somewhat comforted by the presence of her friend Elaine by her side. They had become fast friends and she had invited Elaine to meet her parents. The three women had talked for a long time about what lay ahead of the two younger women. When Elaine related her story it brought out a side of her mother which astounded Mildred, for anger was expressed by the older woman in a way that she never expected, anger that found expression through a string of choice expletives as the tale progressed.

Now, the two young women walked out of the departure lounge hand in hand to a new world.

That's how she came to be on this bus travelling down Bathurst street.

Mildred felt Elaine tugging at her hand. "Girl where you been? I here talking to you and you ent hearing a word I saying to you. You like you in dreamland."

"I'm sorry," Mildred answered, "my thoughts were back home. It happens like that often, forgive me."

"There's nothing to forgive, that happens to me often too.

I get to thinking about home and it's like I go into a trance and my whole life flashes before me." Elaine answered. "I understand. I just wanted to remind you that I have to get off at the next stop because I have to meet Peter. We close to Bloor. We'll meet later in the evening at Eaton's, so don't spend too much time in Honest Ed's."

"That's okay." Mildred answered, "I'm looking forward to seeing Peter again. Say hello to him for me."

The bus stopped and Elaine got off, waving to Mildred as she pulled her coat tighter around her neck against the cool breeze that scattered the garbage on the street corner, and walked down the street.

Mildred's reminiscences brought Elaine back to the reality of her own situation. As she walked the short distance to the shoe store where she was to meet Peter, her thoughts turned to her own situation—the circumstances that had brought her from her sunny, warm home, to this cold, snowy, windy land, where her loneliness sometimes threatened to overwhelm her. Often, in the stillness of the night, when her employer's snores filled the silence of the night, she remembered home, and she pulled the blankets a little closer and willed her mind to travel the distance back to her home in Chimborazo, back to her son, back to her mother, back to Miss Prescott.

Elaine

Elaine and the sailor moved slowly along the dimly lit corridor. From the doors on either side came the sounds of bed springs creaking in rhythm, a thin laugh from a woman or a man grunting and panting. The other whores were at work. It was a busy time for all of them. An American aircraft carrier had come into port a few hours earlier and over a thousand hungry men, their pockets bulging with money, had charged ashore looking for relief for their sperm-filled testicles.

The whores were ready.

* * * * * *

When the bus left the little village of Chimborazo with Elaine aboard, she did not look back although she knew her mother was standing in front of the house looking at her. She could feel those eyes in the centre of her back; the eyes of her mother and those of the child sucking his thumb and holding on to his grandmother's tattered dress, scars on his skin from the eczema that she had cured by nightly baths in Lysol water were beginning to darken. His belly jutted out prominently, filled with the gas which distends the bowels of the malnourished. Many nights she had looked at the sleeping child tossing fitfully in his bed, and had cried out of frustration. She knew that the restlessness was because of hunger. Her breasts had long since dried up and the 'bush tea' she gave him was often the first and last thing which crossed his lips.

Before his birth, when she used to work at the plantation,

things were different. Every day she and her mother walked the two miles from the tenantry to the plantation fields. They, along with twenty or thirty other women and men of varying ages, walked with their hoes over their shoulders to whichever fields were to be weeded and fertilized with the manure from the stables and cow pens. Their clothes were old and tattered and the women had them tied around their ankles to protect them from the bites of the centipedes. The crocus bags* tied around their waists served to make pads to support the baskets of animal dung which they carried on their heads, and which were natural fertilizer for the fields. Some of the women wore hats plaited out of dried Royal Palm fronds; hats with broad brims which flopped over front back and sides, which, although crude-looking, were functional in protecting those areas in its shade from the heat of the midday sun.

At five-thirty in the morning, as the sun's rays reached toward the sky painting it red, when the air was sweet with the freshness of the dew-wet grass and the blackbirds chirped as they picked the oats from the horse dung in the road, they were all awakened by the sound of the bell ringing. The plantation and its bell governed their lives. It had been so from the time their ancestors arrived from Africa and had been sold to the masters of the plantations. It told them when they were to awaken and it told them when they should cease their toil.

As they left their small homes and started on their journey they called out to each other, summoning them each to join the gang*, meeting those who were getting their water supplies from the pipe* in the village. The pipe was communal. It was a place of cohesion, for everything in the village was discussed by the women at the pipe. They chatted and laughed as they made their way to the fields, for laughter was their means of survival. It was the antidote to their pain and suffering. The road from the pipe would be wet, in even areas, with the water splashing from the cans and buckets or barrels in the cart which the donkey slowly pulled, or from carts with wobbly wheels, home-made carts with paint cans of water, and the girls walked with graceful swinging steps balancing buckets on their heads, the movement of their hips a symphony of rhythm.

Early morning was the best time of the day.

When the gang of laborers reached the fields the overseer would be waiting. He would be sitting on his big black horse, his sallow face burnt by the sun, and the cork hat on his head. His shirt and short pants would be khaki like the cork hat, and he would carry his silver-plated riding crop in his hand. He would be uneducated, or he might have reached fourth or fifth standard at elementary school, but he would be the overseer.

He would be a Bajan white, a 'poor bakra Johnny'*. He would lead the workers to the potato or yam field which was to be weeded, and would sit on the horse all day while the hoes raised into the air and were brought down, dislodging the clumps of black earth to which the weeds clung.

The women and the hoes moved forward, and the horse moved forward too.

When the overseer sent the message to tell Elaine that he wanted to see her, she suddenly felt unexplainably cold. Suppose he was going to tell her that there was no more work for her? Why were the women looking at her like that? Her mother had been sent into another field to work, so she could not ask her what to do. She knew she had to obey the message, but she felt confused. Why had the overseer left the fields and had not come back? As she walked along the cane row which joined the path leading to the house she could feel the eyes of the other workers boring into her back. Her bare feet hesitated as she put them on each step of the verandah which ran along the front of the house. Her knock was barely audible, but he heard it.

He was sitting. He had been drinking. She could smell it on his breath as he opened the door for her to enter, and as he led her to sit in the cane-bottomed chair at the table. The room was scantily furnished; a pine table with two chairs, a two-burner oil stove in one corner, an old refrigerator that rattled each time the motor started, and an old Morris* chair which had seen better days was near the door. The walls were bare except for a picture of an old map of the island. A few dirty pots and plates with half-eaten food were in the sink and the counter next to it and the shelves over the sink had a few cans of soup on them. It was not a nice room.

She looked back, wondering as he locked the door.

"Elaine," he said, walking toward her. "How long you been working on the plantation?"

"Six months, sir," she answered. She still could not figure out what this was all about. She knew that he had to know how long she had been working there. She had gone to him to get the job.

"And this is the first time you ever come up to the plantation house?"

"Yes sir."

She fidgeted uncomfortably. She rubbed the sole of one foot against the instep of the other. Her eyes were downcast and she twisted her fingers around each other as her folded hands lay on her lap. The khaki clad figure came to the table and poured a drink from the pint-and-a-half bottle* into a glass. He added some water from a large enamel cup and gulped it down, coughing as the fiery liquid touched his palate.

"You want a drink?" he asked.

"No please, sir," she answered still not looking up.

"Yes, I want you to have a drink. I want you to see that I am not such a bad fellow. I been watching you a long time, from the time you come to work here, even before that, from the time I see you with your mother when she bring you to help her weed. That is why I give you the job helping her when she ask me to let you help out. You look good, real good. Here have a drink." He poured the glass half full of rum and held it out to her.

"No please, sir. I don't want any. I never drink rum at all. Please, sir, if you don't want me for anything I want to go back to work." She looked at him, her eyes appealing.

"You don't have to worry about working for the balance of the day. I get that fix up. Don't forget, I is de overseer. I can do anything I want around here. Here, drink up." He brought the glass to her.

She turned her head away as the strong smell of the rum reached her nostrils. He brought it closer to her. She felt him grip her, and the smell of the alcohol mixed with the rancid smell of his armpits made her feel sick. He forced her jaws open and she gagged as the drink burned its fiery path down her throat. She tried to pull his arms away. She screamed but it was soundless as the rum shot from her lips. She tried to get away from the chair, but he held her and forced her back into it. Although she clenched her teeth the fingers which dug into her jaws forced them apart and more rum went down her throat. She coughed and some of the liquid ran out of her nose. Tears streamed down her cheeks. She struggled and tried to get away, but he was strong and his arms held her pinned to the chair. His face was close to hers.

"Lissen girl, I been watching you for a long time, an' longing fuh you, an' I going have you. Come, gimme a li'l kiss. I like you an' I would give you anything you want, just gimme a li'l piece."

He tried to kiss her but she quickly turned her head aside. She shuddered as his unshaven face brushed hers. She was crying and struggling as hard as she could, for she realized why he had called her to the house.

Frustrated in his attempts to kiss her, he seized both her hands in one hand and with the other forced her around so that he could grind his mouth against hers. She gagged again as the foul odor of his mouth went to her nerve centers. She tried to turn her face again but his arms were like steel. She tried to rise again from the chair and with a crash it fell under their combined weight as two legs broke off. He released her for a moment as his drink-fogged brain registered that the chair was broken.

"Little Black bitch!" He shouted as his hand flashed to her face with a slap. "Now I'm really going to fuck you good. You got to pay for breaking that chair."

Tears blinded her, and sobs wracked her body as she tried to rise from the floor. The rum she had ingested was making her giddy.

"Please sir, don't try to do that. I not clean. My menses only start day before yesterday."

"I don't want any excuses. I get you here to fuck you and that is what I going do. All you Black bitches walking roun' shaking your asses like the world is yours, looking at me like I is dirt; don't think I don' see it, and all like you, too proud to accept your true station in life. You here to serve we. All you want to do is keep your pussies for all the Black boys and when white men want some, you getting on like you got the crown of the Queen of England between your legs."

Elaine tried to see through the tears, but only felt the hands forcing her to the floor as she tried to rise again. She felt the hand lifting her skirt and almost lost her breath as the heavy body lay on top of her. She felt the hand breaking the string of her cotton panties made from the flour bags her mother had obtained from Miss Taylor's shop and had washed and bleached, and felt the same hands pulling at the bloody strips of cloth that served as a sanitary pad. She tried to squeeze her legs together but a knee ground into the muscle, causing her such intense pain that she was forced to open them. And all this time she begged and pleaded and cried.

The weight on her chest became more suffocating as he lifted his hips to slip off his pants, and then she felt him fumbling. She became aware of a new object.

He tried to enter her, but couldn't. He forced her legs further apart, used his fingers to guide the object, and with a lunge tore into her. He was inside.

She was a virgin. Pain; intense, nerve-pinching and unbearable pain forced her mouth open and stopped her breath. Her eyes rolled, her fists clenched and blood appeared in her palms as her fingernails punctured the skin.

And then a scream rushed from inside, wrenched from the very roots of her being. It was a single scream. It was the scream of Africa torn from its roots, raped and plundered.

And then he was thrusting, and thrusting. His beard scratched her neck as he buried his chin in the hollow between her neck and shoulder, and his behind worked like a piston. Thrust! Thrust! Thrust! Every stroke made the pain more severe and every thrust was a knife stroke to her heart. He was panting, and perspiration fell on her face. At last with a grunt, he discharged. She felt the spurts of warm liquid enter her womb.

He rolled off. His penis and the blond hair around it were bloody, and blood and semen dripped from his now flaccid tool.

She stopped crying. Tears no longer came. They wouldn't come for a long time. She was no longer a virgin.

When she looked around he was lying beside her, sinking into sleep. Before she could get up, a snore broke the silent air. She looked around at the blood on the floor, on her legs, on his groin, on his sprawling legs, on the overturned broken chair by his head, and it sickened her. She felt the bile in her throat and could not stop the vomit.

She wished she could vomit herself to death. She felt dirty. She looked at him, helpless and at her mercy, and wanted to kill him. She wanted him to die. She wanted to die.

She crawled to a window, and by degrees, got out and jumped to the ground. She felt the sharp stones bite into her legs and bleeding palms as she fell. She got up, and with slow steps, limped into the cane field which ran along the back of the house. The cane blades cut her arms and face as she pushed through the high stalks, but she knew this was less painful than having to meet anybody. This way she could get home without being seen. Time and again she fell as vines running along the cane ground tripped her. Her heart was heavy with shame.

Which man would want her now that her maiden* had been taken—taken by force by a white man?

She finally reached the paling which formed the division between her house and the next. There was no gate, only a division, a space left out. In this village, like all the others around the island, there was no need for gates. All were the same and there were no barriers between them. They shared a common heritage and a common destiny. There was no one to keep out, and no one to let in. All passed freely.

 She went through the yard and, passing through the shed-roof* of the little chattel house, fell on the grass-filled flour bags which served as a mattress. She closed her eyes, and soon merciful sleep embraced her and soothed her in its lap of unawareness. She was like this when her mother came home from work long after the sun had set.

The gentle sound of her mother softly singing while she rocked her to and fro awakened her. Her head was on her mother's lap, and the tears from the old woman's eyes as she gazed unseeingly into the distance fell drop by drop on the young girl's face, as if to wash away the pain. She realized that her mother was singing a song which she had taught Elaine many years before. A song which had been handed down through the generations, from the days of slavery.

She was singing in Swahili. The only other time Elaine had heard her mother sing it was when her great grandmother had died. She had taught it to Elaine's mother. The song had given their ancestors comfort on the slave ship and soothed them in their moments of greatest pain during those traumatic weeks of the Middle Passage when they had been torn from their roots and, shackled together, tossed on the wind-swept ocean.

At night on the rolling ships these songs provided counterpoint to the drumming of the waves against the sides of the ship and they survived.

As she gazed at the older woman's face she saw more than sorrow. Carved into the ebony were tolerance, compassion, understanding, grief, love and sympathy. Carved into it were centuries of endurance and suffering which, however, could not remove the softness of love nor dim the passion to withstand in the face of each new trial. She saw and understood who she was.

Her mother was Africa, ravaged, torn, plundered, but still standing proudly and withstanding all that had been done to it. She too was Africa. Their feelings were the same.

Her mother detected the slight movement, and without stopping her rocking, drew the young girl closer to her breast.

"I understand chile. You ain't got to say nutting, I know what happen. Some people still living in the time when they bring your great-granny, an' great-gran pappy in chains to sell pun de wharf. One of these days vengeance going come. I will never forget nor forgive what was done to you. I will make Juju and call on the great Dumballah, and the Orishas, and the spirits of your ancestors, to bring justice to you and vengeance on his head. He will pay! He will suffer." Her voice trembled with the strength of her feelings, and her eyes flashed like points of light.

For a brief moment Elaine wondered how her mother knew what had happened to her, but then she understood. The Wind listened to everything. It heard and whispered to the trees, which spoke softly to the canes which rustled their blades in reply. The laborers heard and understood, and the hoes rose higher and carved the black earth a little deeper in hurt and anger and frustration, and each downward stroke was a blow at the overseer, and the black earth understood, and it was not angry with them.

It was thundering and raining when Elaine felt the first

pains. They tore through her swollen belly with the sharpness of the lightning which pierced the sky and preceded the crashing thunder. The old windmill where she had sought shelter from the sudden storm gave her some protection. The matted tangle of weeds overhead, so thick that no sunlight came through, protected her from the strong wind and steady downpour which, in a short time, turned the paths up the hill into rivulets carrying the black earth into the gullies. She knew that her time had come and she was afraid. She didn't know what to do. Her house was over the other side of the cotton fields where she had been picking cotton, and she knew she could never make it through the tall stalks and mud. The old windmill was closer.

A flash of lightning revealed the stooped figure in the familiar straw hat coming up the steep incline toward the windmill, and she knew that everything would be all right. She relaxed, and when the next flash of pain came, she was glad.

Her mother had found her. She would be in good hands now.

Elaine awoke and felt the warmth of the small body moving next to her. She felt the warmth of the sun which was shining with renewed brilliance. The sky which she could see through the opening was blue and cloudless, and the air smelled with the freshness which comes after a tropical storm, bringing with it a headiness and lightness of spirit. The storm clouds were gone.

The older woman was standing at the opening of the old windmill, her face blending into the shadows of the brick, both of them ageless and strong. She stood gazing out over the hills across the steady line of breakers coming in to the shore. She gazed toward Africa, and seemed to be asking each breaker for the message it had brought from across the ocean to deliver on the shelving sand.

And the message came. A message of birth and rebirth. A new Africa was born. A sign of hope and strength, a new spirit of pride and industry. A continent, a people, a baby. And Elaine looked at her son and smiled. She knew that he was a new generation. He would be different. There would be changes.

Her mother came and took the infant. She went to the opening and, holding the baby in both hands, held him aloft, showing him to the mother country and offering him to her. A fresh wind was blowing gently, steadily; a bridge across an ocean from a continent to an island. It was the chain which linked the people. It was unbroken, blowing straight from Africa. There was nothing to get in the way.

******

She had stopped working in the fields. She was never working in the fields again. After her episode with the overseer she had become hardened.

She felt that all white men were the same. And she wanted to punish every one of them for what the overseer had done. She kept those thoughts of revenge in her breast for many years. She was going to use them. She was going to hurt them. She was going to be a whore.

The hotel on Bay Street was not far from the Bus stand, and when she got off the bus it was just a short walk to get there. She reached the door, went in, and walked straight upstairs.

As she entered the door she remembered a phrase she had read in Dante's *The Inferno*, during the period of withdrawal she had imposed on herself after the 'incident' with the overseer, and she wondered if her situation was not the same. In her mind, she was about to cross the River Styx. The oarsman had brought the boat to the shore. She had stepped ashore and passed under the sign: *Abandon hope all ye who enter here.*

No! She would never abandon hope, and she would escape from this hell she was about to enter and deny the devil her soul. It might take a long time, but her son needed her, and she was prepared to spend some time in hell with the devil to get him the things he needed. After all, the act which created him was her initiation into hell. She had thought a long time of her manner of revenge. The overseer would be taken care of by her mother's prayers to the Orishas. She would take care of her revenge on other white men. Her final decision was not haphazard.

Her steps slowed on the first few steps of the staircase. A small band was playing a Tommy Dorsey tune, and she heard the voices of people upstairs in many conversations at the same time, competing with the music. She steeled herself and moved up the stairs.

******

Between the time of his conception and the first few years of her son's life, Elaine kept very much to herself. She was no longer the bright jewel in the village. She became withdrawn, and even when her girlfriends came to see her, she didn't talk much. She no longer smiled, and when the villagers passed on their way to the pipe or to Miss Taylor's shop at the corner, they could see her head through the window, buried in a book, reading. She was always reading. It had become a passion with her. There seemed to be urgency in her now, a determination in her movements, and a fire burned in her eyes which stopped anyone who tried to carry on a lengthy conversation with her.

After the birth of her baby she refused to let anyone look after him. Even her mother found it difficult to communicate with her, but the older woman understood.

She was the topic of conversation at the shop for a long time. Everybody knew everything, but they knew nothing. They could never be part of her thoughts, and they could never understand the hate that was burning inside. Sometimes, when she gazed into the distance, it seemed as if a glaze came over her eyes. It was as if she were summoning the heavenly hosts to be her defenders. It was as if she was willing them to do her bidding, and the villagers became afraid for her and worried about her. Everybody who lived in the village and some who didn't had an opinion.

"Miss Taylor, please to trust me with a gill of lard oil, half ounce of cooking butter, and a half pint of rice. I got to get this li'l food done 'fore that no-good man of mine come in from work." Miss O'Neal said to Miss Taylor one Saturday morning, and then opened the subject of Elaine's condition once more.

"But you see Elaine condition? It seem like she going off she head. All she doing is reading, reading, all de time. She don't know so much reading could sprain she brain."

"I don't know chile," Miss Taylor answered. "Since that episode with the overseer the chile isn't the same. One time she smile would light up the whole village. I used to like when she come in the shop, she was sprightly, always had some joke to tell. She could imitate anybody and would make me laugh till I cry. Now to see she does bring tears to my eyes."

"That's true," Miss O'Neal answered, shaking her head. "She was real lively. She ain't the first the overseer do so, but she take it real hard. She was always different from the rest of the girls though. Some of them get on like it was a privilege to go to the overseer house, but not her. She didn't knock she self 'bout, and no man couldn't come with no freshness to she. She always tell me: *Miss Taylor*, she always call me Miss Taylor, she was always very polite. *I not letting no man come and wash himself up on me. I am keeping myself for my husband. I want to lead a decent life so that my children will be proud of me and have more than I ever had. They got to get education in their heads, because education is the way to get out of these fields. My children not going labor all day, in the hot broiling sun in those fields. They going get education and work in offices, and wear collar and tie, or they going be doctors or lawyers. They are not going to be tending no stocks or cutting pond grass from the hedge row. No Miss Taylor, they going lead good lives. They got to have education. Somebody can take away your money, or your house can burn down, an' you lose everything, but once you got education in your head, nobody can't move it. My children got to get what nobody can't take away. Education is the key.*"

"What she say is true, you know," Miss O'Neal answered. "That girl real sensible, she does think deep. I did always like her and like to hear de way she does talk, not great like, but she does speak proper English, and sensible. Old as I is I does learn a lot from listening to that girl talk."

Miss Taylor shook her head sadly, as she wiped the cou-cou stick* with butter on it on a piece of paper, plopped the paper into the tray of the balance scale, and watched it descend.

"She used to come and talk with me for hours. She used to tell me all 'bout she hopes and dreams. That girl had ambitions. Now all she doing is drawing up in the house. She ain't got nothing to be shame bout. It isn't she fault that the system so onfair that you can't even bring up these white people before the judge, 'cause if you do, you not going get no satisfaction. White people bring we here and rule everything an' dey does get on like dey can't get punish. But the Lord does prevail." She raised her fist and eyes heavenward.

"Amen!" Miss O'Neal answered, nodding her head vigorously in agreement.

"But you see wha happen to de overseer?" Miss Taylor continued, "I always say God don't like ugly. You know onfairness don't prosper. He tek advantage of that sweet innocent young girl, an where dat get he? Tell muh!"

Miss O'Neal shook her head in agreement. She, like everyone else in the village, knew what had happened, but she wanted to hear it again from Miss Taylor.

"I know something bad woulda happen. As soon as I hear wha he do to Elaine, I say: *Lord have mercy*, an' I hold my belly, because I know something bad was going to happen. I know dat she is one girl he should not have interfered with. She mother learn all the secrets from she mudder who come straight from Africa."

"Something bad?" Miss Taylor continued, "It worse than that. He might as well be dead. It was the said same day that we had that big able thunder storm. The said same day that Elaine give birth to she chile. He was out in the field when the storm come. The thunder was rolling and the lightning was flashing, and the rain was pouring down and everybody coulda see that God was vex. All the people in the field pick up their hoes and move on home. They know God was vex. The overseer was on the horse when de rain start, and for some reason the animal would not move when de overseer was ready to go home. He just stand up in the middle of the field with he legs plant firm in the ground, and all the overseer lick he, he would not move. He stand up with his ears prick straight up, like he listening to hear some thing, and he feet plant firm like the cane stalks. And then the overseer get real vex, and get off and start licking the horse some more with that silver-handle riding crop. And the animal stand up and take all the licks without moving, with he head hold up high, big and Black and strong, taking all the licks, like we ancestors who come over pun de slave ships, and he not moving. He eyes wide open, and he nostrils flaring, and he looking at the overseer, but he not moving. And all this time the thunder rolling an' the wind blowing hard like it talking and quarrelling, an' de rain was pouring down, an' everybody in their house shut up tight, and praying. And the overseer soaking wet and the horse not moving. So then the overseer start to walk back cross the field, slipping and sliding in the black mud and falling down in the cane holes, and all he doing is swearing and he nasty and he clothes full of mud. Sudden so a big bolt of fork lightning zigg-zagg cross the sky and strike the silver-handle riding crop, and he light up like starlight on the fifth of November. He let go one big able scream, stand up straight, trembling from head to toe, and then fall down, Bram, and the horse still ent move.

Then the storm finish and when the people come, the overseer was lying down the same place, he eyes wide open, and he didn't know nobody, an' he clothes burn up and smelling real bad. When the people get there the horse was standing up the same place, but he was real calm, and when the people carry way the overseer, he take he time and walk right in the stable, like nothing didn't happen. And you know what else strange? Every now and then he does look cross by Elaine house, and whinny, like if he telling she: *everything all right now*.

The overseer ain't talk since, and he still the same way with he eyes wide open up to now. He can't say nothing, even though you can tell that he know what going on. He just lying down on he bed an' it is de same Black people dat he tek advantage of all dese years dat got to clean he up. He can't do nothing for heself. That is retribution."

Miss O'Neale let out a sigh as if she had been holding her breath the whole time Miss Taylor was talking.

"I agree. That is retribution. The ways of the Lord are passing strange. Do good and good will attend you."

"Amen to that." Miss Taylor echoed. "That man ain't no more use to heself. He might as well did see the girl an' leff she. As I say, onfairness don't prosper. He that knoweth the way of the Lord and doeth it not, will be beaten with many stripes."

"Praise the Lord." Miss O'Neale answered as fervently as if she had finished praying in her church. Miss Taylor finished wrapping the small packages neatly and entered the cost of the items in the little exercise book she kept for all the customers who credited from her. She always noted the amounts and totaled them carefully, but she never asked them for the money. She trusted them, and they trusted her. She knew that when they had the money they would come and pay what they could.

That was the way they lived in the village.

Many of Miss Taylor's customers would come into the shop early on Saturday mornings on their way to town to sell the ground provisions that they had grown on their small plots of land. They would leave the list: 'half gill of lard oil, 2 oz. cooking butter, 1 pint rice, 1 lb. sugar, half pint split peas, six cents in biscuits, quarter pound flour', enough to feed the family for a week, and when they returned in the evening the items would be neatly parcelled out, wrapped in paper, and placed on the counter where they would be picked up.

That was what kept it harmonious; a circle of trust. The overseer broke that circle. He was punished. The village would never be the same again. It was beginning to change, and that change started with Elaine. She would never trust again. She decided on her method of revenge for the hurt and the indignity she had suffered at the hands of the white overseer. It was carefully thought out. It was different. It was radical. It was psychological.

******

Elaine was sitting in a corner of the large room which served as a bar, dance floor, and lounge at the hotel. It was a hot August afternoon and business was slow. There were no ships in the harbor and no sailors to provide clientele for the whores. She didn't mind though. She had her books, and as long as she had them she was happy. She could immerse herself in them and dream her dreams.

She could feel eyes on her and when she looked up, she saw Mrs. Prescott looking at her. Mrs. Prescott was the proprietress of the hotel and looked out for her girls, protecting them from the more aggressive sailors, and maintaining order in the establishment. She was quite large, and, as she had showed a few burly sailors, rather strong. She had descended from among the red-legs* of St. John, who could trace their ancestry back to the indentured servants brought over from Scotland and Ireland when the island was being developed. They were the white counterpart of the African slaves, except that in the early days, although they could get into the church, they were forced to sit in the back rows. They thus became known as back row Johnnies, later corrupted to bakra Johnnies.

Mrs. Prescott was kind, and from the beginning had been touched by the young girl who had come up the stairs of the hotel and said quite simply that she wanted to work there. She was touched because she saw something in Elaine which was not present in the other girls who worked there. There was nothing harsh or raucous in her manner. She always dressed neatly and stylishly, but never flamboyantly. She never cursed or swore, and didn't drink alcohol. However, she seemed to become completely detached when she went with any client, as she called her customers. It was as if she turned off a switch which removed any emotion or feeling from the sexual act. She lay in the bed as if she were lifeless.

Often, completely dissatisfied, sailors cursed and swore and some wanted their money back. Each time she calmly looked at them and said, completely emotionless and expressionless,

"You got what you paid for, sex. You didn't buy my emotions or my feelings. No amount of money can buy that. You wanted sex, and you paid for it, and you got sex. You can't get your money back."

And while the naked man sat on the side of the bed, usually with a shocked expression, she would wash herself, calmly dress, walk out to the hotel verandah overlooking the street, and commence her reading.

They called her the Ice Maiden.

The other whores couldn't understand her though. They felt that she should 'show more respect to the white sailors, after all, they spent good American money', and 'it wouldn't do no harm to be nice to them'.

She ignored them.

Motherly Mrs. Prescott understood, though. She knew that this young girl had been hurt and that this was her way of seeking revenge, but it was bad for business. Dissatisfied customers had a way of giving a place a bad name. Elaine would have to go, but she knew what she was going to do. She sent one of the girls to call her.

Elaine entered the room Mrs. Prescott used as her office, although it was just a corner of her living/dining room. She wondered what the problem was.

"You wanted to see me Mrs. Prescott?"

"Yes, Elaine, come in and sit down."

Elaine sat on the edge of the chair facing the older woman. The wind blew gently through the window ruffling the beaded curtains which hung from the door jamb. They made soft tinkling sounds as the strands brushed against each other. It was almost musical, and soothing.

Mrs. Prescott looked at her for a long time. She felt love for this young, beautiful girl. She had known many women who came to her establishment, but this one was different. This one was special.

"Elaine," she said gently, "this work is not for you. Your heart is not in it. Why do you do it?"

"I need money for my child. He has to get a good education." She spoke defiantly, and almost angrily, but her voice betrayed her.

"No, Elaine," Mrs. Prescott answered gently, "you know that's not the whole truth. You could make more money by being nicer to your clients. You act as if you are angry, as if you are seeking revenge. You want to hurt. You know that to hurt a white man's ego, especially his sexual ego, and to frustrate it is the greatest revenge."

Elaine turned her head, and looked out the window. She looked out over the shimmering emerald blue waters of the bay where the wavelets were creating tiny breakers as they came in over the little reef which guarded the small beach behind the hotel, the beach where she went every morning and swam, and lay on the white sand, letting the warmth of the sun soak into her body. She looked out over the water, but she did not really see it. It was as if a shade was pulled over her eyes.

"Tell me about it." Mrs. Prescott's voice was so gentle it seemed as if she hardly spoke. It was hypnotic.

Elaine looked at her and started to speak. The dam burst, and like a river in flood, the words flowed. The years of pent-up emotion gave way and as she spoke the older woman felt the tears welling in her own eyes, and dropping on her ample breasts. Tears also started in Elaine's eyes, and her sobs increased as her body released the tension which had been bottled up inside for years. She recounted the rape by the overseer, and the birth of her son, and the hatred she felt and the desire for revenge that was never satiated and which had consumed her all these years.

Mrs. Prescott came to her, and just like her mother before, held her close to her bosom; a picture of contrasts, this beautiful young Black woman and the white matriarch. She held her there for a long time, long after the sun had set. She held her there until the young girl's body was no longer wracked by sobs, held her until her body was relaxed, held her until she knew the poison was out of her system. She would no longer hate.

"Elaine," Mrs. Prescott said finally, "I'm going to help you. You will not prostitute yourself any longer. The government is offering courses at the Housecraft Center to prepare young women to immigrate to Canada. I am going to get you into that course, and then help you to go to Canada. I will ensure that your son has everything he needs until you can send for him."

Elaine couldn't believe her ears. Mrs. Prescott was giving her the opportunity she needed. She could go to Canada, she could further her education, she could realize her ambition— she could become a teacher. She could become somebody. She would have a future. Her son would have a future. She could become anything she wanted to be.

As she embraced the older woman she smiled, for one of

the few times since *that* day. She laughed, and Mrs. Prescott laughed, and felt good because this was the first time that she had heard the young girl laugh. It was a bell-like laugh, and revealed a different side of the woman. It was a good feeling. Elaine, she thought, was a gem. All she needed was the chance to be polished to shine. She would get that polish in Canada.

Elaine was glad she had met Mildred, for as their friendship grew she realized that she had found a true friend and that their destinies seemed intertwined. Mildred gave her the self-confidence she needed, and gave her the assistance as they studied together to overcome the hurdles of her limited education. She was a fast learner and Mildred was patient. She made good progress and was especially proud of the certificate they all got, certifying that they were trained domestics, eligible to fulfill contracts with wealthy employers, after which they could become 'landed immigrants' and stay in the country. They could become upwardly mobile.

The bus from Bathurst and Steeles turned into the station, bumped across the intersecting streetcar tracks, and jerked to a stop with a hissing of air brakes. The driver opened the doors and the rush of winter wind made the passengers pull their coats tighter around their necks. A light snow began to fall and the darkening skies were a portend of a heavy snowfall before the next morning. As she descended, Mildred paused slightly and looked around the station.

For weeks the young man had been staring at her and she eventually found her slight annoyance replaced by curiosity, so much so that she looked forward to seeing him. She had decided to find out about him and why he was always looking at her so intently. *Who was he?* she wondered. He looked Barbadian; he was always neatly dressed, and never seemed to be waiting on anyone. She would find out today, she thought, and then fate intervened in a way she least expected. Elaine's friend Peter appeared and shouted his name: Harold. With a slight glance at him she hurried out the door. Peter knew

Harold. She would get details of him later.

Harold

Harold felt his body traveling along a long tunnel which, strangely, was not dark, but seemed to have a suffused light about it. He heard a voice in the brightness calling his name. As he drifted further into the tunnel toward the light, the voice became more distinct, and more insistent.

"Harold, come, we are waiting for you."

He found himself resisting and trying to reverse the drifting of his body. It was almost like swimming against a strong tide. He tried answering the voice, but it was as if a heavy weight was on his chest, making breathing difficult. He struggled and eventually managed to scream out.

"No! No! I'm not ready yet. I can't come. I've got things to do. Why do you want me?" He heard his voice echoing down the long tunnel. He tried harder to fight the tide carrying him toward the light, and the voice. Then it seemed as if he began to make progress against the tide. He began to go back, out of the tunnel. The voice in the light seemed to answer him.

"All right, you can go back. We're not quite ready for you yet."

He felt himself drifting back out of the tunnel, but it seemed as if he was coming out through the side, and up through the earth. As he drifted up, he soon heard other voices and gradually became conscious of people around him. He opened his eyes and blinked at the bright lights shining around and in them, and as they became more accustomed, he saw the masked and gowned figures hovering around his bedside. He became aware of the many tubes and solutions running into his arms, and then he understood what they were saying.

"Good, he has regained consciousness. For a while there I thought we had lost him." The masked figure hovering over him looked at the beeping monitor. "His blood pressure is up and his pulse has steadied. We had better give him another pint of blood to be certain."

He turned away and started to remove the gown and surgical gloves. Harold became aware of the figure behind him which now leaned forward, removed one of the bags whose tube ended in his arm, and replaced it with another.

"We did lose him for a while." She said, "It's a good thing that he is strong and healthy. He really took a battering."

At first Harold couldn't understand what they were talking about. He had no idea where he was except that he was in a hospital. He tried to look around. She placed a cooling hand on his forehead.

"Don't try to move." Her voice was calm and reassuring. "I'm Dr. Cowley, the anesthetist. You are in the recovery room of Notting Hill Hospital. Everything will be all right now."

His head felt heavy and his thoughts were hazy, but as they wheeled him out of the room it all came flooding back in a rush of memory.

Along with the mental and physical pain he remembered the police whistles as they came charging into the fighting Blacks and Whites. Was it his imagination that they seemed to be separating all the Blacks and raining blows only on them with their batons, asking no questions, just beating, beating, beating, unceasingly, beating, beating, and beating?

He couldn't recall how many blows he received about his head and in his ribs. He only knew that he was hurting and hurting, and then the hurting stopped. Blood was flowing from his head. Blood was flowing on all sides. And the noise, the swearing, the cursing; West Indian, Bajan, Jamaican, Trinidadian, Cockney, English accents all mixed into one sound.

And the fighting continued. Bodies clashing, stabbing, cutting, fists, knives, stones, garbage cans, chains, sticks, bottles, everything. All across the street, all around Notting Hill was in an uproar. It was a riot at Notting Hill.

Like an earlier riot in Bimshire.

Harold fought, hitting out at every white face which appeared in front of him. Every white face had to be an enemy. He hit at it with his fists, he kicked, and he used whatever he put his hands upon, whatever he had, despite the blood which was gushing from his head, until he lost consciousness.

Now, in the hospital room, he touched the bandages around his head, looked at the blood running into his arms, looked at the other bags with their various liquids, smelled the almost overpowering smell of the disinfectant strong room, and he remembered. As the memories came back his anger grew. He hadn't done anything wrong. He and his friends were defending themselves.

They had left the pub early, long before closing time, and were on their way home. They were in good spirits, and as usual they were arguing loudly. No group of West Indians, especially if it has Bajans in it, argues about cricket quietly. It must be loud, done with fervency and passion, and must include gesticulation. Cricket, by the West Indian, must be played the same way, with passion and verve.

"Man I tell you nobody can't bat like Gary Sobers. I wasn't in Jamaica physically, but I was there in spirit. I saw every shot that he made when he made that three sixty-five. The announcer on the radio didn't have to describe the square cut for me to know it was going straight to the boundary. And when he talk 'bout a cover drive, I know that not a man move before the ball hit the boundary. Gary is the greatest batsman in the entire world."

"Don't forget that three sixty-five was not out and he would have made more runs too, but the crowd invaded the field as soon as he broke Len Hutton's record." Another voice interjected.

"He make runs, but he na cyan bat like George Headley, mon."

Bruce was a Jamaican, and he never let the Bajans forget that Jamaica also produced great cricketers. The argument, although loud and accompanied by the appropriate gesticulations, was good-natured. As they turned the corner, they came face to face with the Teddy Boys lined up across the road. They stopped.

"Oi, monkey face, why doncha go back where you came from?"

They were all dressed alike—black leather jacket and pants, heavy steel toed boots, shaven heads, and studded belts. Each held a weapon in his hand.

"Oi, nigger, we don' wancher heah. We don' like your kind." another proclaimed with a sneer.

"You don' see no coconut trees around here do yer?" another one asked rhetorically.

The group of Black men stood looking at them. There was no fear. They just stood looking, together. The tension began to build.

The Teddy Boys felt it. They breathed it and they realized that they were going to have a fight on their hands. This group of Black men was not going to run like others had in the past. Harold had decided long ago that he was not going to run from any of them. He had stopped running when he boarded the SS Surriento in Carlisle Bay and left Barbados. He was through running. All of the others were of the same mind. They too were through running.

Harold looked around for a 'Bajan Missile'—a big stone. He reached down and pulled up two of the cobblestones from the edge of the road. Peter, his best friend, clenched his fists. He didn't need any weapons. He was big and strong. Bruce, from Trinidad, took off the cover of a trash can nearby, and at the same time, reached into his pocket for the switchblade knife he always carried. Its click as it came open was loud in the stillness of the windless night. Donvil, a big Jamaican, took up a piece of pipe which was lying against the trash can. Each of the others armed himself with a bottle or whatever else was available.

Not a word passed between them, but they were thinking as one.

Then they advanced. Silently, steadily. Straight ahead.

The Teddy Boys didn't move, but shifted nervously, swinging the bicycle chains and gripping the pieces of wood and pipe in their hands a little tighter. They were a little less brave now. The Blacks moved forward. Together. Shoulder to shoulder. West Indian unity in the face of adversity. Like the cricket team. United. Island differences forgotten, facing battle as one. West Indian Boys [were] marching. The war was on again. Grim-faced, they moved forward toward their destiny, like the 'Light Brigade'. And in the face of this determination the Teddy Boys began to understand.

These were not Asians or other weak-kneed immigrants. These were West Indians. Unafraid. Willing to fight. Willing to die, if need be, but they were not running. There was no moving back. Forward ever, backward never.

The tension in the air permeated the walls of the buildings nearby and the shifting of blinds in the windows, behind which some of the faces could be barely seen, indicated that the occupants were aware.

And they clashed, and stabbed and beat, and fought. And all the anger and hate of the colonial system, endured for all the years, all the deprivation which had forced them to come into exile, the insults, even anger at the cold hostile weather—everything—came rushing to the surface of their collective consciousness, because they were from a common root, a common heritage, a common background. Everything for them was the same, though they were separated by sea, and different. They were West Indians. They were One. One people, One Nation. And they were unafraid. Moving forward. There was no moving back. And the anger exploded against the Teddy Boys.

And the Police came and other West Indians came and the riots began at Notting Hill.

The nurse came into the room and took his temperature, wrote the results on the chart at the foot of the bed, fussed over his bandages for a short while, smiled at him and quickly left the room. She was quietly efficient, and she was West Indian.

Harold gazed through the window and then closed his eyes as a tear coursed down his cheek. He drifted on his thoughts back to the beginning, back home. He remembered home.

＊＊＊＊＊＊

It was hectic in the small chattel house perched on the brow of the wind-swept hill which afforded a breathtaking view of the entire east coast of the island. The aroma of cakes, sweet bread and chicken, all baking at the same time, it seemed, set the taste buds to salivating and the mouth to watering. People kept coming and going in never-ending activity. Everybody seemed to be talking at the same time. Harold was going away. He was going to England.

This was the biggest thing to happen in the village since Mr. Drayton, at the age of seventy-four, had taken a thirty-two year old town girl for his bride. The entire village had turned out to witness the ceremony at the little Church of the Nazarene that Saturday afternoon.

Of course all the young men wondered enviously how he had been able to get such a 'nice-looking, big-botsy* woman, with such nice bubbies*'. They wondered if he could last through the honeymoon. The women expressed the opinion that 'she only want he for the little money and piece of land that he got', that 'she only waiting for him to dead, to get a young man', and that soon 'he would get a big horning* from some young fella'.

After the excitement of the wedding day everybody in the village had some of the food, because Mr. Drayton made sure that a lot of food was cooked. He killed two of the big sows he had, about twenty chickens, and had the baker busy with all the baking that had to be done.

Everything soon settled down, especially since he not only survived the honeymoon, but moved around with more vigor, and Jessica, his wife, showed everyone that she really loved her husband. She kept his house clean and neat, made sure that he appeared in public well-dressed, and openly lavished her affection on him. From the sounds that came from the bedroom, all could hear that she was also well satisfied in that department. The houses were too close for the sounds not to be heard, and besides, Jessica was a shouter. There were no secrets in the village. In fact there were no secrets in any village on the island.

Harold came out of the drawing room which faced the winds coming from Africa. It wasn't yet dark, and as he sat on the step, he looked at the view before him. He had done this many times as he was growing up, lost in the solitude of his thoughts, wondering about his future, wondering about the people across the heaving ocean, wondering about his ancestors. He was always wondering, always dreaming, always thinking.

Now, once more, he looked at the deep aquamarine of the water close to the white sand, and the deep, almost black, heaving ocean further away giving continuous birth to the breakers coming to the shore. This was the ocean he was going to cross. These were the waves he would have to rise above. This was the turbulence he would have to battle against shortly, and survive.

As he sat on the step and looked ahead, his thoughts drifted back.

He had been a bright boy at school. From elementary

school he had won a scholarship to Harrison College, the top secondary school on the island. From early he had developed an affinity for mathematics and science, but he especially liked chemistry. When other students rushed to get through their experiments, he was methodical and precise, getting top marks consistently.

As time passed his sensitivity increased and his awareness of other facets of life at school became more acute. He became increasingly aware of the segregation, self-imposed or otherwise, which was a daily occurrence at this elite school. He noticed how the white students always congregated together at lunch time. He noticed how the better-off Black students congregated under the Sandbox tree by the clock tower. He noticed how the poorer Black students scattered throughout the grounds at these periods playing games.

He became aware that this society within the high walls of the school was a microcosm of the island which divided itself, or was divided by others, not only along racial, but also class lines. He became aware of the prejudices among the staff. He noticed how teachers coming from England, even those without certified accreditation, discriminated against the Black students and the few Black teachers. His resentment grew against the curriculum, dictated in England, governed by England, enforced by England, with examinations set in England by Englishmen, and corrected in England.

Everything was England and English. There was English history, English grammar, English literature, and English language. You could never get your School Certificate unless you got a pass in English Language, even though you might get distinctions in everything else.

They never taught Black history. They never taught about Black people, or Black heroes, about Black achievements, or about Black warriors. They never taught anything positive about Blacks, or even your own country. Even when you spoke your dialect, you were chastised for speaking 'broken English' and that was bad. It had to be discouraged and stamped out. One had to speak 'proper English'. Yet this was a country that was predominantly Black. This was a school that was predominantly Black.

Of what significance was the Battle of Hastings to a Black boy in the island? Who cared about Queen Boadoecia? Who cared if Julius Caesar came, saw, and conquered the Saxons? What about the Moors? What about the history of the island? Where were our heroes? What about the Riots? What caused them? What was their significance? Who was Bussa? Who was King Ja Ja? Where did he come from? What about slavery? What about it?

As he became more aware, Harold's resentment grew. He became more argumentative, more withdrawn. It seemed that, as his consciousness grew, his desire to excel grew in parallel. His intention and goal became the winning of a Barbados Scholarship. This would be his way of escape.

As he saw the favoritism shown to the white boys his intention to succeed became an obsession. This was reinforced on that fateful day, the day of the inter-school sports. It was a day he would never forget, a day etched into the chemistry of his brain. The competition between the Secondary Schools was fierce.

The rivalry between Harrison College, Lodge, and Combermere, created great excitement. They were close together in points, and any one of them could have emerged victorious. All through the day fortunes shifted between them and the air was charged as the final race approached. The outstanding athlete at this competition was a student from the Lodge School. Crichlow was a gifted sprinter who seemed to float on air as he ran, and the general feeling was that he was good enough to qualify for the Olympic Games.

The final race of the day, upon which the championship would be decided, pitted Crichlow against an athlete from Harrison College, a white boy of German parentage who had come to spend a year at the school prior to returning to Germany. The four hundred and forty yards race was Crichlow's best distance, but Von Klaus was fast. He had easily won the two-twenty yards race earlier in the day. At the gun Von Klaus opened a five yard lead, and all eyes focused on him and Crichlow. The other runners soon fell behind, and the yelling and screaming grew in intensity to a thunderous din as the runners rounded the final turn. Crichlow cut into the lead, and as they straightened for the final hundred yards, he accelerated past Von Klaus and won the race comfortably. Lodge School had won the championship. The students from all the schools were yelling and screaming and jumping up and down, because what mattered most was that Crichlow had won, and had also set a new record. The athletes congratulated each other.

Von Klaus extended his hand to the victorious Crichlow, who shook it in acknowledgment. Then Von Klaus, after shaking the Black champion's hand, wiped his own on his shirt.

The cheering ceased abruptly. Kensington Oval was silent as a funeral. That single act killed the spirit of victory. It killed the spirit of harmony. It reinforced the structure of the society.

Harold never forgot that moment.

******

The kerosene oil lamp in the little house burned late into the night, every night. Long after the village had gone to sleep, that light shone like a beacon on the hill. People down on the beach could look up and know that Harold was studying. They knew he was going to get the scholarship.

Everybody knew he was the brightest boy at Harrison College. And the time for the examination came, and he knew that he had done well. Everybody knew. And the results came back from England. And a white boy got the scholarship. But

Harold knew the scholarship should have been his. He knew. Everybody knew. There were no secrets on the island.

Even the headmaster knew that Harold should have received the scholarship, but, as he said, it was out of his hands.

And Harold's resentment against the system grew, and his resolve intensified. He would win in the end. They couldn't get the better of him. He was brighter and smarter than any of them. He redoubled his efforts.

One day he got a call to report to the headmaster. As he approached the door to the office with trepidation, he wondered what had happened. He couldn't recall anything he had done wrong, and he only had a few weeks left at school. He knocked at the door, and the gruff voice behind it answered:

"Enter."

As he entered, the body behind the voice turned to him.

"Ah Watson, come in and have a seat." It said, indicating a straight-backed cane-bottomed chair in front of the desk. Harold sat gingerly on the front of the chair, nervously twisting his fingers around each other. Mr. Harmond's desk was the epitome of disorder. Nothing seemed to be in place, and when he rested his arm on it, books and papers fell in confusion to the floor. Mr. Harmond made no effort to pick them up, in fact, he seemed not to notice, he continued talking as if nothing had happened.

"Now Watson, you know, and I know, that you should have gotten that scholarship."

The memories of his disappointment which had been quiescent resurfaced and quickened Harold's heartbeat. Mr. Harmond continued:

"I know how disappointed you were, we all were, but that is the way of this world we live in. You must see that as a challenge to rise to higher heights."

Harold began to fidget nervously. He knew that once Mr. Harmond launched into one of his lectures it could go on for a long time, but he wanted to leave. There were things he wanted to do before he went home. He had to finish some chemistry experiments, and there was a passage from Caesar's Gaelic Wars which he was to translate from Latin to English. The voice droned on:

"…and therefore one must not let disappointment prevent one from pursuing the path to success. As a consequence, knowing your interest in mathematics, I took the liberty of asking a friend of mine, one of the old boys, to give you a chance in the accounts department of The Bank. He has agreed, and wants you to come and see him next Monday morning."

Harold couldn't believe his ears. Was Mr. Harmond in his right mind? No Black people worked in that Bank in any post other than as messengers.

"Excuse me sir," he began tentatively, "are you sure he knows who I am?"

"Oh yes, I am sure he does. I described you as one of the brightest boys in the school." Mr. Harmond answered.

"But sir, did you tell him where I am from?"

"Of course, Watson. I do know where you are from, you know. I recommended you very highly. Just be sure you are there early. Good luck, my boy, the job is yours. Give a good account of yourself." And he started to laugh heartily at his own pun. "Ha! Ha! Ha! Get it Watson? Good account. Ha! Ha! You are going to be an accountant, going into the account department." He convulsed with laughter.

Harold got up and exited in confusion, leaving Mr. Harmond to his laughter. Here was Mr. Harmond telling him that he was going to get a job in The Bank, in the accounts department. Something was not right.

When he told his mother, she was overjoyed. His father had died when he was seven years old, and his mother had raised him single-handedly, although much of his training and upbringing was under the tutelage of Joe the joiner, who was his mentor and taught him everything he knew. His mother was overjoyed.

"Oh, Harold, that's the best news we've had in a long time. You'll be able to save the money to go to university."

She treated his going to university very matter-of-factly, as if it were a very natural thing. As far as she was concerned, it was already ordained. He paced up and down the small drawing room.

"Mum, it just doesn't feel right. You know this society. They'll never give me that job. You know that no Black people work there in any clerical positions, and for me to enter there in the accounts department, even as a trainee... They'll never accept that. This whole thing doesn't feel right."

His mother, on the other hand, was quite stoical:

"Never mind Harold, put your faith and trust in God, and whatever He does will be well done."

Harold didn't say anything to her, but he already knew what God would do. Didn't He do it to him already, with the scholarship?

Early on Monday morning Harold arrived at The Bank. He had dressed carefully, and couldn't help but be happy at the way his mother fussed over him, straightening his tie, brushing off the non-existent lint from his carefully pressed serge suit. She herself had gotten up before he was even awake and polished and shined his shoes until they glistened in the morning sun. Joe came and gave him advice on how to conduct himself at the interview.

As he left to catch the bus, she stood at the door looking out after him. When the bus reached the top of the hill, he looked back and she was still standing there. He wondered how long she stood there after he had gone. He felt her prayers following him all the way to The Bank.

As he walked into the imposing edifice on Broad Street he felt his heartbeat quicken in anticipation of the interview. He tried to think of the questions that could be asked, and formulated the answers in his mind.

His first inkling that things were not right was when he

approached the secretary's desk outside Mr. Arther's office. The sign on his door said Chief Accountant, and his secretary was placed in a strategic position just outside the door. You had to get past her to get into his office. She was white, as expected; a Bajan white. He noticed the thinness of her lips which, combined with flashing eyes and the set of her mouth, conveyed the impression that she was angry.

This impression was reinforced when he spoke to her and gave her his name. Although he asked very politely, if he "could please speak to Mr. Arther, because he had an appointment with him", her demeanor reinforced the initial impression that she was angry. It was as if she were angry because he had dared to come in The Bank and speak to her. She curtly told him to have a seat and, taking up the phone, spoke softly, but her words were audible to him.

"Watson is here to see you Mr. Arther, he says he has an appointment, but I don't have it on my appointment book." The voice at the other end was speaking. Finally she simply said "Yes sir," put down the handset, and turned back to her work without saying a word to him.

She is angry. He thought. Why? Was she angry because he was Black? Was she angry because she had to talk to him?

He gazed around the office, noticing the old photographs with the name plates indicating past presidents of The Bank. They were all Englishmen. A buzz on the secretary's desk brought him back to reality. Mr. Arther was ready to see him.

"Go in," she said, not even bothering to lift her head. She just pointed to the door to her left.

Harold walked past the dark mahogany door into the book-lined office. Mr. Arther sat behind a large imposing desk of dark mahogany. He was bent over the papers he was working on, and did not look up right away. When he did look up, his expression visibly changed. Harold knew immediately. His senses had been so finely tuned in anticipation of the event that he knew. Mr. Arther remained seated.

"Who are you?" He asked curtly.

"I am Harold Watson, sir, Mr. Harmond the headmaster made the appointment for me to see you. It is about the position of Trainee Accountant."

"There must be some mistake. When I spoke to Harmond about the position, he said that he would send me his brightest student."

Harold could feel the resentment and anger building inside.

"I am the brightest student," Harold answered quietly, but emphatically, and with assurance.

"But you're Black." The words were out before they could be recalled. "I can't give you the job."

Harold felt the bile rise in his throat. He knew he was going to be sick. He turned and ran from the room. He didn't stop running until he reached Queen's Park, almost a mile from the bank. He went down to the trash houses* near Spartan Pavilion. No one was around. It was calm and peaceful there. He sat on the step and began to cry. Thoughts rushed through his head like the fires through the cane fields, blown by the wind, consuming everything in its path.

It is unfair, he thought. He couldn't help being Black. That's just how it was. This was a country of Black people. What had he done to be punished this way? He had never done anything wrong in his entire life. He believed in God; a merciful God, a God who rewarded those who were good. This was the message which had been taught to him for his entire life.

But God was punishing him. Because he was Black? But didn't God make him Black?

He stayed in the park for the rest of the day.

When he finally reached home it was dark. His mother was waiting for him at the door, as if she had not left the spot since he had left that morning. She knew. Mothers always knew.

Wordlessly, she put his dinner on the table and sat silently across from him at the table while he ate. Tears rolled down his cheeks, and the food stuck in his throat. He looked at his mother and said, in anguish,

"Mum, why am I Black?"

"You are who you are," she said quietly. "You are made by God. You are a good boy and I love you very much. Never question your color or let it be important in your life. Be who you are and want to be. Be proud of yourself and your achievements, and always be the best that you are capable of being. Your color will only be important to those who are less than you in ability, and they are not capable of hindering your progress. God has something else in store for you, so do not let this event deter you from reaching your goal."

She came around the table, put her arms around him, and drew him close to her as the sobs shook his body violently. She understood his disappointment and hurt. She knew this was only the beginning. She understood, and she kept holding him tightly to her body. The love flowed out of her body and into his. He gradually relaxed and fell asleep in her arms.

She remained like this, deep in thought, looking over the hills to the breakers, foaming white in the silver moonlight, rolling into the surf. The wind whispered quietly through the trees. It heard. It had been in The Bank, and had listened to everything. Now it spoke softly to her. It reassured her, it strengthened her. She got the message. He had to escape.

The next day she had a long talk with him. She had come to a decision. Workers were being recruited for the London Transport system—bus drivers and conductors. She had a second cousin living in London who, she was sure, would take care of him. She would write and ask that favor of her. While working with 'the transport' he could continue his studies. It was settled.

She got a loan from the government. The chattel house was put up as security, and Joe also signed as a guarantor. Joe spent many hours with him giving him advice on how to handle the many challenges he was sure to face. He even spent time teaching Harold how to fight, even though his mother frowned upon it. She kept silent though, because she knew that Joe was doing it in Harold's best interest.

Now, as he sat in the darkening evening and looked over the ocean he would soon cross, Harold wondered. Would he ever see this place again? Would he ever see his mother and Joe again? Would he ever return to this rock, in this wide heaving ocean? Should he go, or change his mind even at this late stage? One thing he knew for certain, nothing would be the same once he left. He would never be the same again. Ever.

Morning came too quickly. Everybody in the village came to wish him goodbye, and they all stood in the road and waved as he left in the rickety old truck that Mr. Jones used to haul sugar canes to the factory. His suitcases were packed to the brim with sweet bread, cakes, baked chicken, flying fish, and everything his mother and the rest of the village could put in.

Everybody gave something. Even Mr. Drayton came and brought a heavy winter coat, smelling strongly of moth balls. He had used it many years earlier in England, after serving in the war. It was well preserved, like its owner. That was the way they lived in the village. Everybody gave something to someone else. They shared everything: hopes dreams, feelings disappointments, and grief.

When they finally arrived at the baggage warehouse, they saw the steamship which would carry him away from this land of his birth like those other ships so long ago. It was Italian: the S.S. Surriento.

The place was a mass of confusion. Hundreds of men, women and children jammed the shed from which they would board the rowboats to take them out to the ship in Carlisle Bay. Men, women and children were crying. Some were to part forever.

The time for him to board eventually arrived. As he embraced his mother he felt the tears start. He couldn't help it. She was dry-eyed, but he knew her heart was heavy. When she silently took the necklace with the shells and seeds from around her neck and placed it around his, he felt her love more poignantly than ever before. That necklace had been her mother's and her mother's before that. It had come over from Africa with the slave ship. It was a link. Eventually they all had to let go.

As the row-boat pulled away from the pier-head he kept looking back, his hand on the necklace, until their faces were indistinguishable.

He climbed the gangplank, but instead of going to his cabin, remained standing by the rail. He felt the trembling as the steamer got under way, and saw the water, beaten into foam by the propeller, leaving a wake as the bow moved through the unbeaten water ahead. He remained standing at the rail looking in the direction from which he had come. He remained there for a long time. His island was gone. He was going into exile. He felt more lonely and alone than he had ever felt in his entire life. He pressed the necklace closer, and felt more comfortable. His mother was with him.

He was on his way to his cabin when he heard a faint sound coming from under the stairway he was about to climb. He stopped and, looking into the semi-darkness, saw a young woman seated on a box, crying.

"Hello," he said quietly.

"Hello," she answered hesitantly.

"I know how you feel." Harold said. "I feel the same way too. I wish I could cry though, but all I have is this lump in my throat. I can't even swallow properly. What's your name?"

"It's Maureen. Maureen O'Neal." she answered, wiping her eyes with the tiny handkerchief she had crumpled into a ball in her fist.

"Hello, Maureen O'Neal, my name is Harold Watson. Please stop crying."

"Okay," she said, wiping her eyes once more. She felt comforted by this tall, handsome young man who seemed so self-assured and warm. She felt less alone and lonely in his presence. He sat beside her on the box. They talked for a long time, scarcely noticing the passage of time lulled by the dull sound of the engines pushing the ship inexorably forward toward their destinies.

They went to supper together when the ship's bell rang loudly, interrupting their conversation. After that they were together constantly. They ate meals together, and spent hours on the deck talking of their hopes and dreams.

She was going to England because she couldn't get a job after finishing her education at St. Michael's Girls' school, one of the best on the island. She had decided to go, like so many other girls from secondary school, to study nursing. She didn't want to leave home, but there was no other alternative.

There was no future in the village, or, seemingly, on the island, with its prejudice, discrimination, and lack of opportunity.

The resilience of youth soon pushed their loneliness into the background, and they began to enjoy their journey as the days passed. And then a single event brought them back to the reality of their situation. One of the passengers, a young man, had become seasick from the first day at sea. He was constantly vomiting, and nothing the ship's doctor could do helped him. Six days out to sea, he died. The Captain sent a telegram to the family. They would have to pay the cost of keeping the body on ice until they reached port, and then pay the costs of shipping the body back home. The reply came back. They had no money. They had sold everything to get money for him to emigrate. Even the house was owned by the government. He was buried at sea. He never reached 'the motherland', or returned. His exile was permanent. Perhaps he reached his own promised land. Did he believe in God?

Often, after that, Maureen and Harold stood together at the bow of the ship, holding hands, and looking toward the approaching land they couldn't see. Their future was ahead. They arrived in London on a cold, dark, foggy, rainy evening. Right away Harold knew. He knew that this was not the motherland. This hostile land, with its hostile weather, and hostile people, could not be the motherland. A mother protected, comforted, and gave warmth. A mother guided and nourished her own. This land gave no guidance, no direction, and no warmth. You were on your own. You found your own way.

So many of his fellow passengers, men and women, arrived without sense of direction. They had no idea where they were going, where they were staying. They were lost. There was no one to meet them, no one to guide them. This land was alien.

It had been a long journey by train from Italy where the ship had docked, and everybody was tired, hungry, and mostly discouraged, and cold. Very cold.

His mother's cousin met him at the station. She had received word of his coming and was prepared to welcome and house him. All she needed to know was that this was her cousin's son. She had been in England for many years. She didn't have much, but she was prepared to share what she had with him. The umbilical cord was long. It was never broken.

The first few weeks he was there she and Harold talked for hours. She was glad for his company, and like all exiles, wanted to hear all the latest news from home. She wanted to be home through him, to see the village through him. She never seemed to tire of asking him about this person or the other, to hear about the happenings in the country, and what changes were taking place. It was the longing, the longing of the exile.

He renewed his acquaintance with Maureen who had gone on to her nursing school in Croydon when they had parted at the train station. He visited her some weekends. It was a good friendship. They were comfortable together, taking long walks in the countryside, and sometimes, indulging in tender love-making, but they both knew they wouldn't marry each other. They were good friends.

He quickly became accustomed to his new surroundings and his new life. His good academic record, the recommendation from Mr. Harmond, as well as the Pastor at his mother's church, combined with a shortage of qualified persons, enabled him to get a job as a chemistry technician in a research laboratory.

He soon found out where the nearest West Indian cricket club was, and gravitated toward it. The cricket club was home. That's where the boys were.

In the village back home, the pipe was where the gossip and news were disseminated. You got your information from the pipe. Here the cricket club was the pipe.

He was invited to join, and that's where he spent many of his free evenings—on the field, going to the pub afterward, getting involved in lighthearted, loud raucous, arguments, the lifeblood of West Indian males who argue constantly about cricket, and having a good time.

The atmosphere in the Pub that evening was cheerful. His club had won an important game, and they had gone there for their arguments and pints. It was this evening that he was part of the riots at Notting Hill.

Here in the hospital, he returned to the moment. He picked up a newspaper which one of his friends had brought for him, and as he glanced through, he saw an advertisement and knew right away. There was a job advertisement from the University of Toronto, for a Research Assistant in the Biochemistry Department. He had the necessary experience and qualifications. He knew what he had to do. He believed in fate, and felt that this was the path he was destined to follow. He was going to Canada.

He arrived in Canada on a cool autumn evening and felt an immediate affinity for the country. He completed his passage through immigration quickly and passed over the threshold into his new home with the 'Welcome to Canada, Mr. Watson', ringing in his ears. Officials from the University met him and took him to his temporary quarters at one of the University's dormitories, his home until he found his own apartment. He soon found his way around and into the West Indian community.

******

Harold was in the barber shop across from the subway station when the bus from Bathurst and Steeles came in. He had been waiting anxiously for it, and could hardly keep his eyes away as he watched through the large plate-glass window of the barber shop. The conversation which was going on around him barely registered. With a start, he realized that he was being spoken to. One of the regulars, George, a fellow Bajan, was light-heartedly teasing him.

"Man, Harold, staring out the window is not going to make the bus come in no quicker. Come an' fire one with the boys."

Harold glanced around at them, but just as quickly turned his attention back to the window with a brief comment.

"No, you guys go ahead. I'm not in the mood for that right now. Maybe I'll join you later."

George turned to the barber, who was busily clipping a customer's hair. Next to him, on the counter amidst the scissors, clippers and combs, was a bottle of rum, some cokes and some glasses. He stopped clipping, and took a sip from a glass half filled with rum and coke. He was also Bajan.

"Tony," George said, "help me with this man. He need help."

"Come on Harold man," Tony said, "every Thursday for the last four weeks, you been doing the same thing. You stare out the window, and as soon as that Bathurst an' Steele bus come in you run outside, go in the station, look at the gal, and then come back in here. If you like the gal, go and tell her. She can't kill you."

"Except with looks," George interrupted, "I see some of these chicks give some cut-eyes* that could kill. Some of these women got a way of looking at you that does stop you dead in your tracks if you try to make any improper advances."

"That's true," Tony the barber answered with a hearty laugh. "But the gal that Harold got his eyes on wouldn't do that. She look refine. And she look good too."

"Man, you can't trust no woman," George replied. "How much more dangerous than a serpent's bite is the cut-eye* of a Bajan woman?"

George was always coming up with these witticisms which were obviously his own inventions. Harold ignored them. Today was the day. For weeks he had been watching the Bathurst and Bloor Station. All the men used to watch the Bathurst and Bloor station on Thursday afternoons. That was when the girls who came over to work as domestics got their day off. They always met in the station, to renew acquaintances, exchange news, gossip, and draw strength from each other before going to Honest Ed's to do their shopping.

This weekly meeting was important. It was the link with the past; to the old days of the meetings at the pipe in the village. Some of them met their boyfriends in the station, and while those who had none eyed them enviously, they would either go downstairs to get the subway downtown or they would get the streetcar to go to Jew-Town to buy their meat, salt fish, or other groceries. Afterwards they would go to the boyfriend's apartment for the rest of the day and night. In many instances these apartments would be in the basements of the houses among the heater pipes and furnaces, or in the attics.

Harold had decided that today was the day he was going to make his move. For a whole week he had rehearsed exactly what he was going to do, and what he was going to say. For weeks she had consumed his thoughts.

He remembered the day he first saw her. He was in the barber shop, just like now, reading a two-week old Advocate newspaper which some new arrival had brought into the shop, when he looked up and there she was. She had just stepped off the bus and was walking into the station. He stared. She was the most beautiful woman he had ever seen. She was elegant, stylish, and walked with a regal bearing. She had class.

Harold knew love. He knew that he wanted her. He knew that there was no other woman for him. And then she was gone, hidden from his sight by the other waiting women who immediately surrounded her, talking excitedly. She was obviously very popular.

He was at the barber shop early the next Thursday, and the next, and the next. And every time he saw her, he knew. This was it. This was the woman for him.

One Thursday he got the courage to go into the station and stand by the door as she passed through. He smelled her perfume, and then she was gone. But her voice lingered in the air, like her perfume. It was sonorous, musical, and cultured. She spoke 'good English' as she chatted with the other girls, but there was no 'putting on airs'. She was in place with them. They were one, united by a common circumstance, seeking the same goal: success.

Their intention was to put up with the hardships, the insults, the loneliness, and any and everyything to make a better life than they had back home. And they met in this subway station even though they were from diverse backgrounds. Until years later.

This station was a hub in the life of the West Indian exile in Toronto. It was the center for renewal of memories, the connection to one's roots. It became, temporarily, very temporarily, home.

Streetcars from downtown which passed the Canadian National Exhibition grounds terminated there. Streetcars left there and traveled up Bathurst Street for some distance, then turned on to St. Clair Avenue. A lot of West Indians lived on, or off, St. Clair Avenue. The Bathurst Street Bus traveled up Bathurst street, past Avenue Road, through the heart of the Jewish section where so many Bajan women worked as domestics, and up to the new suburbia of Steeles Avenue.

The Bathurst and Bloor Station was also a hub for all those

other immigrant shoppers: Greeks, Italians, Portuguese, Europeans, and sundry others who used it to get to Honest Ed's to buy cheap goods. That was all immigrants and recent arrivals could afford. Honest Ed became very rich.

After Elaine left, the now crowded bus seemed to crawl along the street. Mildred was becoming impatient. She kept looking at her watch, shifting her grip on the bar of the seat in front of her on the crowded, swaying bus. It was finally nearing the station.

Harold was in the station standing in a very strategic position, backing the plate glass window to the street of the subway station. It was a position from which he could observe everyone who got off the bus or came up from the subway. They had to pass through the doors he was facing. He was going to talk to her today. This was it. Today. Definitely!

The bus turned into the station. His eyes, fixed on the door, saw her as she alighted. She stood out like a beacon among the other passengers. She was dressed in a translucent, orchid-colored blouse, which contrasted with the white skirt, which fitted closely to her well shaped body. Her feet were encased in brown boots, calf length, ridged with white fur, which enhanced the brown stockinged legs. As she stepped down, her tan-colored camel-hair coat blew open, revealing all this to him. But in that split second, he also saw her breasts, outlined in their lace brassieres, pushing against the opaque blouse.

She was indeed beautiful. There was a pristine purity to her beauty. Her finely chiseled features, full, well-shaped lips, moistened with just a touch of lip gloss, balanced by a hint of makeup on her cheeks, could have been used by any fashion photographer. Her firm up-thrust breasts complemented a small waist which flowed into well-contoured hips and a firm bottom.

He stared, his heartbeat increasing involuntarily. Today had to be the day.

She came through the door and he stepped forward to

approach her. He started to speak. His jaw dropped, and the words were on their way from his vocal chords when the voice came, loudly, unwanted.

"OH SHITE! HAROLD? HAROLD WATSON? What you doing here boy?"

The words went back down Harold's throat, as the new voice bounced off the walls. He knew that voice. He turned.

Everyone in the station turned toward the voice. There was only slight interest though, because everyone knew that Bajans greeted each other that way when they met after a long separation, and they knew it was Bajan because the accent never leaves. It was natural, unrestrained, and honest. It couldn't be quiet. Harold knew that voice. He and Peter were side by side, and then back to back, on that fateful evening at Notting Hill. And then she was gone. Harold looked around, and she was gone. Out the door as if taken by the wind.

"Harold man, how you? Boy is a long time I ain't see you. What happen since I last see you? I thought you was dead. You just disappear from London, and nuhbody din't seem to know where you went to."

Harold buried his disappointment at not talking to his lady beneath the joy he felt at seeing his friend again. But why did Peter have to come up the stairs from the subway, as if he were rising from the grave, at that precise moment, that same day? Why?

Peter had been one of his closest friends in London. He was big, strong, loud, fun-loving, and was only serious about his friendships, his Blackness, and his women. His last memory of Peter before he became unconscious was seeing him, with a Bobby under one arm, and a Teddy Boy under the other, crashing their heads together.

Blood was running down his face, and three other policemen were hitting him with their billy-clubs. He was like Samson, battling the Philistines. Standing tall and bloody among those who had fallen. Peter was strong.

"Shite, Harold, talk to me nuh. We not friends nuh more? You look like you see a ghost, but I not no ghost. I here in the flesh, though I can't say the same bout you. You look pale. I hope you not using no bleach to turn you into no white man."

Harold reached out and embraced the huge body. He couldn't even get his arms around the broad shoulders.

"But Peter man, I must look like a ghost, 'cause I thought I was seeing one just now. Where you come from? You living here? I thought you were dead or locked up. Since that evening at Notting Hill I haven't heard anything about you or see anybody that knows what happen to you."

He was genuinely pleased to see his friend, and his lady faded from his consciousness.

"I living here now." Peter answered excitedly. He seemed as glad to see Harold again. "Look, let's go some place and fire a drink, and catch up on old times. I really thought you was dead. The las' time I see you, you had blood all over, but you was going down fighting. Man you was fighting bad, bad."

"Talk 'bout yourself. You kick some white ass that evening."

"All uh we kick white ass. They thought they could play round West Indians; specially Bajans and Jamaicans? We don't walk bout looking for no trouble. We could live quiet and peaceful next to anybody. We does do we own thing, and enjoy we music, we women, and other people women. And we does laugh loud, even at weself. But we does get real serious when people try to onfair we. We does get real dread. But we show them. God blind them! We show them!"

Peter's brow furrowed and his eyes flashed, at the memory of Notting Hill, but it quickly passed, and he was his smiling, laughing self again. Harold could see that he was anxious to talk about the past and catch up on the period when they were apart. Besides, now that his lady was gone, he had the entire evening free.

"Alright, let's go. I know a little place just past Brunswick Avenue where we could go. It's near Rochdale College. It isn't too bad, and the drinks are not expensive."

They exited the station and, turning left at the junction, walked up Bloor Street past Rochdale College with its huge bronze statue of a nude, hunched over figure: 'the statue of the unknown student', strategically placed at the entrance. Rochdale was symbolic of an era. It was the experimental college of the University of Toronto, where the students could study whatever subjects they wanted, live as they liked, study as they liked or if they liked, and sometimes even taught themselves. There was no formality about Rochdale. This was the time of the Hippies, and drugs, and Yorkville. The time of Jimmy Hendricks, and Woodstock, and the Beetles, and Yoko, and John, and Crosby, Stills, and Nash, and Trudeau, and Freedom. That's what, eventually, caused its demise. Too much freedom. The inhabitants of Rochdale became too drugged, on drugs and freedom and women and sex and disregard for the law, and discipline, and society. And society curtailed that freedom and closed it after many battles. It became a resting place, a home for old people.

Everybody came down to Yorkville. Soon the rich came to be part of the scene, and the coffee shops made more money, and then the rich people bought Yorkville and made it too expensive and decent for the hippies, and Yorkville became something else. It lost its essence and became a spoilt jewel-bedecked member of the establishment, decent and respectable. It lost its freedom.

Harold and Peter reached their destination, talking and gesticulating along the way, filling in the cracks they had fallen through on their way to this new place, country, home. They entered a small coffee shop and took up positions by the window, which gave them a view of the busy street. Each ordered a beer and then began to recount the events which had taken place since they had last seen each other. Peter was voluble in recounting what he had been through.

"Man, Harold, you know, after the riots, they took me to the station. I was beat up real bad. Those policemen didn't want to take me to the hospital. Those sons o' bitches."

"But how they could do that? I remember that when I last saw you, you were bleeding real bad."

"Yes, but they were real vex because I beat a good few of them. Anyhow, the Inspector made them take me there and get patch up. Then they charge me with felonious assault, and put me in prison. The case got thrown out when it get before the magistrate though, for lack of evidence."

"You had it tough." Harold said, with understanding. He knew the English society and its hypocrisies.

"The tough part was losing my job after," Peter continued, "I was fired because I had taken part in the riot and had missed time from work. How de hell I could go to work when I was in prison? I didn't mind though, because when that foreman tell me I could go home, all the shit I had to swallow for all the years since I went there, all the pride I had to submerge because I was in his country, all the years of suffering and deprivation I had to go through, man it just spilled out. When that limey told me I was fired it all came out. I was going burst his ass, because the blood fly up in my head, but one of the boys look at me and shake his head, and I didn't bother. Instead I give him a good Bajan cussing. I lambaste his ass. I let go some rassholes, and God-blind-you's, and tell him what and what he could do with his kiss-me-ass job, and which part he could stuff it. I didn't spare him. I cuss at the top of my voice so that everybody could hear. I cuss his mother, his father, his country, his Queen, everybody till I was satisfied. All he could do was stand with his mouth wide open. It felt GOOD. Believe me, when I walked out of that foundry, and came into the sunshine, I heard birds singing for the first time. I felt like a load had been lifted from my shoulder. Above all I felt like a MAN."

Harold shook his head in agreement, and took a long drink from his glass. He understood Peter's feelings. They were the feelings of the exile.

Peter continued his narrative.

"It was a good thing though, because I soon got a job on a ship coming here to Canada. When I got to Montreal, I signed off and applied for landed immigrant status, and here I am. But what about you?"

"Oh, there's not much to tell." Harold replied. "I too had to go to hospital although I wasn't charged. I had a couple of broken ribs, a severe concussion, and other serious injuries. I almost died. While I was in hospital I saw a job advertised at the university here, my application was successful, and as you say, here I am."

"But what you doing in the Bathurst station? You live near here? Wait, don't tell me that you checking out those chicks who come up on the domestic scheme. I hope you not interfering with mine." Peter was smiling with mock seriousness.

"I live off the Danforth, near Pharmacy Avenue. But now I know why you were coming to the station." Harold answered, slapping Peter on his shoulder, "You came to check out the chicks too. You sly dog. I was about to talk to one of the most beautiful women I have seen in a long time, and just as I open my mouth to speak, you come up the stairs. By the time I look round again, she gone. I was real disappointed, but at the same time I was glad to see you."

Peter started to chuckle, and then his broad shoulders started to shake with his laughter.

"I know who you talking about. Her name is Mildred. I see you watching her with your tongue hanging out as soon as I hit the stairs. It's true, she real beautiful, and you not the only man that would like to get up to her, but she real special. She doesn't mess around. I could introduce you."

"WHAT?" Harold's exclamation was so loud that many of the patrons looked around at the two of them. "You know her?

You could introduce me?" He couldn't believe his good fortune or hide his excitement.

"Yes, man," Peter answered, "she and my girlfriend came up on the same plane. They are good friends and they working as domestics with some white people in the Forest Hills area and Bathurst street. They all come down to do their shopping every Thursday."

"I know, 'cause I been watching her every Thursday for the last four or five weeks, but I have not had the courage to talk to her yet. She seems unapproachable."

Peter reacted with surprise.

"First of all, I never knew you to be afraid to approach any woman. Next thing, she is not as you think she is. She is not unapproachable, but she just carries herself with pride."

"She is not unapproachable?" It was Harold's turn to react with surprise.

"No. She is a very nice person. She is very friendly, well-educated, charming, a lot of fun, when you get to know her, and very ambitious."

"I detected a difference in the way she carries herself, as distinct from some of the other girls. She walks with an air of pride and confidence."

"Yes, she is proud, but she is down-to-earth, and not stand-offish. You should see her getting down at some of the dances the cricket clubs keep to raise funds, especially when they play some of the latest calypsos. Talk about movements." Peter obviously admired her tremendously.

"You know, I've never been to any of those dances." Harold seemed ashamed to admit it. "Since I came here, I have been so intent on making a good impression at the university that I have been working overtime on a regular basis, and have not had time to get out and enjoy myself."

Peter slapped him on his shoulder with enthusiasm.

"Well why you don't come next Saturday night? A group called The Troubadours coming up from home, and they going be playing the latest music to come out of Bim. It's called The Spouge and it really putting the island on the musical map. The girls going be there and you'll have a good time. It's going to be in the church basement, you know where it is, just off King Street. Besides, that is the time to meet Mildred, she will be there."

Harold was really excited now. He was happy at having met Peter again, and the possibility of meeting Mildred made him realize that he needed to get out and relax. It had been a period of concentrated and continuous work from the time of his arrival in the country. Finding an apartment, getting settled, becoming immersed in his job, and a thousand other things did not allow him a social life up to now. In addition, the long cold winters only encouraged him to spend most of his free time indoors, reading or listening to music.

"Yes," he said, enthusiastically, "I'll come. What time do they start?"

"Usually around eight o'clock. This isn't like home in Bim. Here, you have to stop serving liquor at one o'clock, so the fellas usually start early so as to sell a good amount of drinks before closing time."

Harold was surprised. "You mean that this is just like England, where they call: time, gentlemen, and everybody has to finish their drinks and leave?"

"Yes, and as a matter of fact, they seem to be more conservative here than in England. You should read some of the regulations they have regarding the transport and drinking of liquor. You're not even supposed to have liquor in the car. If you are transporting it, it has to be in the trunk of the car. More than once policemen have come into the dances to make sure that all signs of liquor are removed by one o'clock. In addition, if you want to buy any sort of liquor to take home you have to buy it from a special store run by the Province. You ever hear anything so foolish? Back home in backward Barbados anybody can go in any rum shop, at any time, and get all the liquor you want." Peter was scathing in his obvious disdain for the liquor regulations.

Harold realized that he had to begin life afresh in the new country. He had to retune his psyche to the new mores and new realities and standards. This is the burden of the exile. He has to start life afresh, regardless of his age. He was really excited now, and he was happy at having met Peter again, and the possibility of meeting Mildred made him realize even more that he needed to get out of the house and relax. From the time of his arrival in the country it had been a period of concentrated and continuous activity finding an apartment, getting settled, becoming immersed in his job, and a thousand other things which did not allow him a social life up to now.

Peter suddenly looked at his watch, and, with a loud exclamation, jumped up from his seat.

"OH SHITE! Look at the time. I promised to meet Elaine half hour ago, and she gets real pissed off if I am late. She doesn't cuss or anything like that but when she gives me 'the look' I know she pissed off, an' I keep very quiet. Look, take my phone number and give me a call, so that we can get together again. Jesus Christ! I gone."

He snatched up a paper napkin, scribbled a number on it, and, stuffing it into Harold's pocket, rushed out the door and disappeared in the direction of Honest Ed's as if the devil was after him. Harold sank back in his seat. He ordered another beer from the waiter, and tried to calm his nerves after the maelstrom of emotions he had undergone in that short time since he had seen Mildred alight from the bus. His heart was beating a rhythm which became mirrored in his actions and thoughts. It was syncopated like the music of his ancestors.

He was going to meet her. He was going to meet Mildred. He said the word over and over. Mildred! Mildred! It was as if he wanted to make sure that it was imprinted on his memory. Mildred! His heart beat faster as he thought of her.

He had renewed his friendship with Peter. He was going to

get back into the Bajan and West Indian social life. He was going to live again. The events which had brought him here were going to be buried. Feelings which had been submerged by the anger generated by discrimination and the struggle to survive in England could resurface. Emotions which made life enjoyable, which made life complete, which had been hidden, could be rejuvenated. Where previously one couldn't freely express one's self on certain topics for fear of repercussions, to the detriment of daily existence, the opportunity was now available to enter into the lifeblood of his West Indian society. Once he got back into his own society, among his own people, he would be free. He paid the cashier and left the coffee shop.

It was late evening, not yet dark, and the fall air was crisp, making his nostrils tingle when he inhaled. He decided to walk to his apartment rather than take the subway as he always did, and as he walked it seemed as if everything was different. He noticed people and saw them as people for the first time since his arrival. Before they were just faceless faces which held no special interest for him. Now he began to see them as they really were: Italian, West Indian, Portuguese, Greek, each different, but the same. They were all exiles, each occupying a different and separate enclave in the city.

As he walked east along Bloor Street he made a mental note to visit the museum and the planetarium as he crossed Avenue Road. He promised to go into some of the stores he was seeing for the first time. He realized that he would have passed beneath them every day and never knew what they looked like from above. He crossed Yonge Street and looked downtown over the heads of the moving, unending stream of people coming and going. He was looking at the artery of the city, a city now finding itself, a city now coming awake, being given life by the exiles. As he passed over the bridge spanning the Don Valley Parkway, he stopped and looked down at the hurrying, scurrying, lines of cars and trucks, going to some destination, all hurrying somewhere.

He walked slowly, deep in thought, past the fruit and vegetable stands on the sidewalk, past the groups of Greeks and Italians sitting at tables drinking or talking volubly, and the little children running or skating along the sidewalks. There was laughter in the air. He reached his apartment building, and as he entered the elevator he felt glad that for once there were no other people. He needed to be alone with his thoughts. He entered the apartment. The room was empty and lifeless. It was a cold room. He suddenly felt lonely.

He had furnished it well. His salary at the university enabled him to afford a nice stereo and television, and the offer of the 'complete apartment, furnished, no-payment-for-three-months' by the furniture store via the finance company, meant that he had everything that he needed. He had money in his savings account and he looked forward to making a down-payment on a car in the near future. But as he entered and looked around there was no one there. He was alone. There was no one to greet him, and no one with him.

He could look after himself. His mother had taught him to cook and wash, and his time in England had taught him to be self-sufficient, but he needed someone now. He needed her. He needed Mildred.

As he showered he had an erection as the memory of her appearance that afternoon returned. He imagined what it would be like to make love to her. It would be heavenly, he was sure of that. He finished his shower and went to bed, but hours passed before he could get to sleep. He tossed and turned, tortured by his need, tortured by his aloneness, tortured by his awakening, his rebirth, tortured by the realization that there was another world, and the knowledge that he needed a woman in his life.

He was also tortured by the memory of his mother whom he had not written to in a long time, but from whom he got a letter every week, and by the realization that she was also alone. He missed her.

He fell asleep promising to write to her next day and send some money. He fell asleep thinking of the dance and the opportunity to see and meet Mildred.

Love

Quite often, when you see Harold and Mildred cuddling in broad daylight, very much in love, you recall their meeting at the dance.

******

It was one of those Indian Summer evenings. The air was just cool enough to be invigorating, and the reds and golds and greens of the leaves on the Maple and Birch trees, falling to form multi-coloured patterns on the carpets of the green grass in the parks, provided the right atmosphere for lovers.

Harold finished his work at the laboratory early and hurried to Bathurst Street. He went into the barber shop early to get a haircut. He wanted everything to be perfect for the evening. Naturally he had to put up with the good-natured ribbing of George and Tony. As soon as he entered George started on him, although he seemed to be directing his conversation to Tony.

"Hey, Tony," he said, without looking at Harold, "You notice that Harold ent been in here for a couple of days now? You think he sick, or maybe he dead from heart affection?"

"I know he love-sick, but I don't think he dead. Somebody would have had to tell we." Tony answered, looking at Harold with a twinkle in his eye.

"Well de way he getting on with that gal, I know he sick in he head." George retorted. He looked at Harold as if he was seeing him for the first time.

"Hey Harold, that's you? You okay? What's happening? I

thought you was dead and I was just saying so to Tony. You not looking fuh de gal no more?"

"You know good enough I was not dead, you bum," Harold retorted with a laugh. "You guys only want to give me a hard time. Here have a drink. I brought some good old Mount Gay rum. That cheap stuff you always drinking bad for your health." He put the bottle on the counter.

"See Tony?" George said, reaching for the bottle. "He sick. This is the first time he ever bring something fuh we to drink. Something wrong." He reached into the small refrigerator which was built into the counter and took out a Coke. He placed it on the counter along with a couple of glasses. They each poured a drink.

"I know something ent right," George remarked as he carefully measured the amount he was pouring into the glass. He used the metal cap of the bottle as a measuring cup, filling it to the top three times, and then a half. He didn't take big drinks, just small amounts often.

"Something definitely is not right, Tony. Harold firing one wid we, an' he ent looking at de subway station. Wha' happen Harold?"

"I came to get a haircut with all the fixings, Tony." Harold answered with a silly grin on his face. "I'm going to a dance tonight, and I have to look special. Tonight is going to be special. You remember that lady I used to admire from this window? The one you guys are always teasing me about? Well I'm going to meet her tonight."

"Shite, man, that deserves an extra drink," George said joyfully. This time he didn't use the measuring cup, he just poured a large drink into the glass, and added some ice, no Coke.

"I glad as shite, 'cause dat mean you won't be blocking up my window no longer," Tony answered good-naturedly.

"Persistence and perseverance pays off, after long and arduous exertion." George was into another one of his homilies.

"Anyhow, we glad for you," Tony said warmly, as they clinked glasses. "I hope she as nice as she look. It's time you had a steady woman in your life. There's nothing better than a human blanket on a winter's night."

"You take care," George added advisedly and fatherly, "Be ye of good behavior and manners. Treat the lady like a lady, and not like a woman, and above all don't get fresh."

The drinks were getting the better of him. He would soon become very Biblical in his conversation before stealing into a corner and falling asleep. This was the atmosphere in the barber shop. It was warm and comforting, very much like home.

Tony finished cutting his hair, brushed him off, and with a kind arm around his shoulders, sent him on his way. He left the barbershop and hurried home with the good wishes of his friends, and lightness in his step.

It was dusk when people started arriving for the dance. The band had not yet arrived, and the disc jockey was playing some soft music on the hi-fi set. The couples there were not yet in the mood for dancing. The members of the cricket club which was hosting the dance to raise funds for an overseas tour back home, were setting up the bar. The secretary was sitting at the door with a small valise on the table, receiving the money from the patrons as they came down the stairs into the church basement.

Harold had arrived early and taken up a position from which he could easily see the entrance and anyone who came down the stairs. He wanted to ensure that he saw Mildred when she came. He bought a rum and coke from the bar and brought it back to the table. A few people tried to make conversation with him, but his demeanor did not encourage long or argumentative conversation, so they drifted off to the bar with their drinks.

He was not aware of their arrival. He had turned his attention away from the door to watch a couple gliding across the dance floor to the music of one of the popular waltzes, when he felt a light touch on his shoulder. He looked around and his mouth was suddenly dry. She was standing next to Peter and another beauty that he had noticed one or two times in the Bathurst station. Peter was smiling as if he had won the lottery. He knew that Harold would have been expecting him to loudly announce his arrival. Instead he had quietly approached and let Mildred touch him. It was effective. Harold was speechless, and his face was a mass of confusion. He attempted to get up from his chair to greet them, and instead of being dignified about it, as he wanted to, he only succeeded in overturning the chair, knocking the glass off the table and spilling his drink and breaking the glass. He was mortified.

Peter laughed out loudly and slapped him on his shoulder.

"It's okay Harold, man take it easy, its only me and the girls, not the police. You don't have to be so scared," and he laughed as if he would never stop.

"I'm sorry," Harold mumbled, as he bent to take up the glass. "You startled me."

Mildred and Elaine were both looking at him intently. Elaine was smiling broadly, because it was obvious that she was as guilty as Peter and was in on the plan to surprise him. Mildred was looking at him more seriously. It was as if she were looking into his mind and analyzing him. A slight smile played around her lips, but he couldn't read the look in her eyes. They were like two bottomless pools of black. Peter broke the spell.

"Harold, my friend, meet Elaine and Mildred. Elaine is my fiancée, and Mildred is her friend. Ladies, meet my best friend, my brother in adversity, and my companion in battle, Harold Watson. I told you about him so don't pay much attention to his confusion. He is not normally like that."

"Hello Harold," Elaine said, holding out her hand. He shook it, her grip was firm and there was warmth in it. When she spoke, her voice was smooth and flowed like the sweet cane syrup from home. "Peter told me a lot about you. I'm glad to meet you," she said quietly.

He turned as Mildred touched him lightly on his shoulder and said: "Peter told me you were anxious to meet me. I'm here now, are you going to welcome me? I'm Mildred."

"Yes! Yes! How are you? I'm glad to meet you. I've wanted to meet you for a long time." Harold's words were not coming out the way his brain wanted his mouth to say them. Mildred solved the problem.

"Why don't we all sit down," she said quietly. "Peter, please get me a glass of orange juice and get something for Elaine too. It looks like Harold was drinking a rum and coke, so you had better get another one for him also."

"I'll go with Peter," Elaine quickly interjected. "I just couldn't trust that man with three glasses, he is so clumsy he's sure to drop one of them." She took him by his arm and guided him to the bar despite his protestations:

"I ain't clumsy. I'll take care. An' besides if I can carry you why I can't carry three small glasses in my hands?" Elaine was unmoved.

"Come, darling," she said, tugging at his sleeve.

Peter went quietly. Harold sat. He was grateful for this respite. His knees were trembling, his heart was beating fast, and a thin film of perspiration appeared on his forehead. Mildred's appearance, her beauty and her very presence had a powerful effect on him.

She was wearing a green woolen sweater open to the vee of her breasts, and a pair of black leather slacks. The open toed sandals with low heels showed her well manicured toes whose nails were polished with a beautiful shade of red which matched her well-shaped fingernails. Her hair was well coiffed and framed her face which had a hint of makeup. Her lipstick matched the colour of her nail polish, with a sheen which gave the impression that they were constantly moistened. She was gorgeous. She put him at ease, reaching across the table and gently touching his hand.

"I'm glad Peter introduced us. I too wanted to meet you. I've been watching you."

Harold was stunned. How could she have been watching him?

"R-R-Really?" he stammered, "Where? When?"

"I know you have been watching me, every Thursday, at the Bathurst station," she replied. "Don't think it is only you men who observe things. I also was interested in you. Not at first, because I wasn't sure you were looking at me, but after a while I realized that I was the object of your attention and I was intrigued. I was flattered by your interest and by your intensity and seriousness. You see, we women also notice men, and the fact that a tall handsome man was so interested in me was very flattering, especially when he chose to stand in the window of the barber shop to see me come into the station. As time passed I made up my mind to talk to you, if you didn't get over your obvious shyness. It was getting to me. Do you think I would have been too bold?"

Harold was getting over his confusion, and her quiet conversation had a calming influence on him.

"No I don't think so," he answered. He had to raise his voice slightly because the music was a little louder. "To be truthful that might have helped to relieve a lot of my anxiety, because I didn't know how to approach you. I didn't want to offend you and spoil any chance I might have had to make your acquaintance. I finally made up my mind to talk to you the day when I met Peter in the station."

"That's interesting," she said, "because I had decided to talk to you that same day, but when Peter came and greeted you, I decided to wait and ask him about you. After the nice things he said about you and the good recommendation he gave you, I agreed to be introduced at this dance." Her eyes softened as she squeezed his fingers gently. "I'm glad I did, now that I've met you."

Harold was thrilled by her touch. He felt comfortable now.

"I wonder what job I can get on the basis of that recommendation." He asked with an attempt at levity. He really didn't expect a reply, and was surprised when she said with all seriousness:

"The job of being with me for a long time."

He was flabbergasted. It was more than he had hoped for. She wanted to be with him. There was no pretense, no hesitancy, she was very straightforward. She was very honest about her feelings.

Peter and Elaine returned with the drinks before he could reply.

"I see the two of you are getting along fine. I'm glad." Elaine said to Harold. "That makes us complete, the four of us. I'm glad we came to the dance and met you Harold, because I have had a hard time keeping up with these two going on and on about you. Peter is constantly reciting your exploits, and Mildred always wanting to know more and more about you, especially after she found out that Peter knew 'this handsome man who is always looking at her in the station', and how 'she wishes he would talk to her instead of just staring' and 'if he didn't talk to her she was going to just go up to him and talk, because if she didn't she was just going to burst'. You can never imagine what it has been like these past weeks."

"I'm glad to meet both of you too." Harold said. "You are both everything that Peter said you were."

The room had become filled with people while they were talking. It was noisy, and the bar was doing a brisk business. The band had arrived and set up and was playing some slow tunes and the dance area was crowded. He felt Mildred's hand on his. "Come, Harold," she said. "Let's dance. I didn't come here to sit."

Without thought of refusal, she came to his side. She slipped her arm in his as naturally as if she had known him for a very long time, and walked to the dance floor. She turned, and just as naturally, slipped into his arms. He was a good dancer and they glided over the smooth surface of the dance floor, seemingly not touching the floor.

Her perfume was heady and when she rested her head on his shoulder, he smelled the shampoo in her hair. She moved easily over the floor and followed his lead effortlessly. Her closeness, the pressure of her breasts into his body combined with the movement of her hips resulted in an erection that, try as he might, he could not control. He was conscious of it and tried to keep her away from him. She also felt it, and rather than moving away, drew him closer, rubbing her pubis against it, and grinding her hips against it. He was in heaven. He didn't want to let her go, even when the music stopped. He knew he would not ever let her go. Not in this lifetime.

And then the band injected a note in the proceedings that reduced everyone to silence, many to tears. They played a tune that became a nostalgic reminder of who they were and where they had come from. It brought them back to reality and reminded them that they were exiles.

> Beautiful, beautiful, Barbados,
> Gem of the Caribbean sea,
> Come back to my island Barbados,
> Come back to my island and me.
> You'll find rest you'll find peace in Barbados....

After the winter's harshness and coldness, lasting many months, this song brought back memories of the place they had left. It was as if a national anthem was being played. Nobody was dancing. Mildred held him close and tears rolled down her cheeks, and she was not the only one crying. The song took them back to their homeland and their collective reasons for their status as exiles.

It reminded them of the many causes for their escape from their homeland and their sojourn in this new 'home', and it brought to the surface feelings that had been submerged under the artificiality of their new life in this adopted country. Minutes after it ended they were still under its spell. Men went to the bar and women suddenly had an urge to go to the washrooms to repair the damage to their mascara, and their souls, by the rekindled memories.

The moment passed and the band began to play a spouge number. The infectious rhythm stirred the genes so that the body unconsciously started to move.

The dance floor was soon as crowded as it had been before with bodies wukking up* as if they were back home, in Queen's park, at the Liberty, or at a social hop* at The Shed* and not in this cold, conservative, white man's country.

Mildred pulled Harold to the dance floor again, and he saw another side of her which pleased and excited him even more than before. She could not only glide across the floor beautifully to a waltz, but when a calypso beat began, her hip movements gave a promise of more to come.

Time passed quickly, and before they realized it, it was time to leave. Harold was surprised that it was almost two o'clock in the morning. It seemed that they had just come in. As they exited onto King Street, Peter and Elaine walked arm in arm a little ahead of them. They were in a world of their own.

"Let's walk home, Harold," Mildred said quietly. "It has been a wonderful night and it's a beautiful morning, and I don't want it to end too soon."

"But where you live up Bathurst street is a long way to walk. We can take a taxi," he answered as he put his arm around her and drew her close. She came willingly.

"I'm not going to Bathurst Street, silly," she said punching him playfully on his shoulder, "I'm going to spend the balance of the morning with you. I'm going home with you. I already told Peter and Elaine to go ahead without me. They understand."

He was ecstatic. It was beyond his wildest dreams.

They walked across Bloor Street, quiet with the silence broken only by the occasional rush of a passing car, contented with each other and their feelings, growing closer as time passed, savoring the peace of the early morning.

When they entered his apartment there seemed to be a different feeling this time. It felt like a home. It was warm. It needed her and it welcomed her. She entered it as if she belonged, as if she knew everything about it.

"Would you like a cup of tea?" she asked, moving into the kitchen. She didn't wait for his answer. It was as if she already knew he would say yes. He removed his jacket, tie and shoes.

"Put on some nice music, please," she said from the kitchen, as she plugged in the kettle. She didn't have to search for anything in the well ordered apartment. She seemed to know where everything was. She seemed at home. She brought the tea to him.

"I put in cream and sugar. I hope that's alright."

He tasted it.

"Yes that's fine."

"Excuse me a minute. I have to go and freshen up a little." She left him, taking her hand bag with her.

Harold was confused. What did she mean by 'freshen up a little'? They had just come in. She took a long time and the tea combined with the evening's events relaxed him. He was sprawled on the couch as the seductive sounds of the music seeped into his mind. When she reappeared and stood framed by the doorway of the bedroom he just stared. She was wearing a diaphanous white peignoir over a matching shorty pajama which hid nothing. Her jutting breasts were displayed in all their glory, evidence of her stimulation showing in the enlarged nipples in the centre of the dark aureole around them. The dark hair covering her pubis stood out in sharp contrast to the white of her attire. Her hips, flaring out from the small waist flowed into well shaped thighs and calves, ending in delicate ankles. Even her toes were beautiful.

She came to him, easily, and naturally, and sank into his arms, raising her lips to be kissed. They kissed for a long time. It was a soft wonderful kiss. When they eventually broke off, Mildred snuggled close to him.

"Thanks for a wonderful evening," she said sighing contentedly. "It was everything I hoped it would be and you are what I hoped you would be."

"No, I should be the one thanking you." Harold answered. "I had dreamed many times, and hoped from the first time I saw you, that an evening like this would take place, but I never thought my dreams would come true."

He gently turned her face to him and looked deep into her eyes.

"I love you," he said softly.

"I know," She said gently.

"I want you very much." It was a simple straightforward statement.

"I know," she answered, "and I want you too. I've wanted you for a long time and as you can see I came prepared. I decided that I wanted you to be mine like I want to be yours."

They kissed passionately, and as he moved his hands over her nipple-stiffened breasts, she put her hand inside his shirt and she played with the hair on his chest. His need for her was overwhelming, but neither one made the move to consummate the moment. It was too beautiful to spoil. They controlled their feelings and allowed the music to cool the fires raging inside. They just lay in each other's arms, contented and secure in the knowledge that their love would create many opportunities for intercourse.

This was not the moment. This was the moment for love.

She snuggled closer to him while he gently stroked her breasts, her legs, and as she opened them, the moisture-smooth opening between them. He held her closer and kissed her gently on her neck. She suddenly gripped him tightly and shuddered. She had an orgasm. A beautiful, quiet, satisfying orgasm. She rubbed her head against his chest and sucked softly on his nipples.

They remained like this for a long time, long after the music had ceased. Her weight on his arm made him realize that she had quietly fallen asleep. He lifted her very gently, and took her to his bed. She shifted briefly when he pulled the covers over her, and kissed her lightly on her lips. He looked at her for a while before turning out the light and returning to the living room.

He was happy. It was a feeling of contented joy. Mildred was his. He had found the love he was seeking. He knew love.

******

You have kept in contact with Mildred and Elaine since that first meeting on the plane back to Toronto when you came to start your new life. Mildred and Sarah have become friends after you introduced them at the real estate course you and Sarah are pursuing. Mildred is also enrolled in the course. You also renew your acquaintance with Elaine when you meet at a house party at one of Sarah's friends. You meet Harold while attending a seminar at the University of Toronto which is affiliated with your hospital. He works as a research technologist at the nearby diabetes research centre. There are very few black technologists at these prestigious institutions, especially at this level of seniority, and it is a natural thing for you to get closer to each other. You all have the same background, trials and tribulations. Through Harold you meet Peter, and you all become good friends, enjoying the sights and sounds of the new city. It has been a natural thing to invite them to your wedding.

All of you have qualities which complement each other. Peter and Sarah work with stock brokers. Elaine works with an insurance company. You are close in every way. Quite often you meet for lunch, whether on the Avenue or in the malls. Elaine's sense of humor and her ability to reduce the most serious topic to the ridiculous is one of the ties that bind everyone closer. Those are halcyon days. They are the halcyon days of the city, the halcyon days of your marriage, and the halcyon days of the country—a country that is emerging from its cocoon of conservatism into the bright light of the Trudeau era. The country is growing.

Mildred and Elaine look stunning at your wedding. Elaine has become immersed in the Black Power movement which is sweeping the continent, and is also influenced by her fascination with the exploits of the Nigerian King Jaja of Opobo, a king exiled to the Caribbean by the British for resisting their attempts to exploit the Palm Oil trade of his country, and who had spent time in Barbados before being sent back to his homeland. He died before he could reach his home again. She has read about the entire episode in a book she borrowed from the library back home. She is dressed in a traditional African outfit which suits her perfectly. Queen Nefertiti has returned.

When she alights from the car and pauses while Peter comes to her side, the oohs and aahs from the wedding watchers make it plain that she is a hit. Peter can hardly stop smiling. Everyone can see that he is proud to be accompanying such a beauty. It is also plain that he is very much in love with her. Despite his size and the impression of brute strength, he handles her with gentleness and looks at her with a tenderness that shows the depth of his feelings. The onlookers have just gotten over the sight of Elaine's arrival when Mildred's limousine drives up. Her appearance reduces the crowd to silence. Cameras start clicking. This beauty has to be captured and retained on film. Harold is ecstatic. He is moving in a fog that seems to envelop him since his meeting with Mildred at the dance.

The strains of Wagner's wedding march reverberate through the church. You turn and there she is, resplendent in her white gown, accompanied by her bridesmaids—her sisters and her best friend—walking slowly up the aisle. Your heart is full, for you have looked forward to this day from the time you met years before, back home. She reaches your side and as you both turn and face the minister, you hear the words which would live with you forever:

"Dearly beloved, we are gathered here today to join this man and this woman in Holy Matrimony. …Whom God has joined together, let no man put asunder."

Everything goes smoothly—the wedding, the photographs, the reception, even the drive to Niagara Falls for the honeymoon. It is the night the astronauts land on the moon. 'One small step for man, one giant leap for mankind'.

You make the leap.

As time passes the family settles into the routine of establishing itself. Your step-children, now part of the Canadian system, quickly fit in and advance through the school system. You realize the need to keep ahead of the game; to remain at the top of your profession. There are few of your colour with your qualifications and experience who have reached your level in this city, but it is necessary to improve constantly. You enroll in courses designed to advance you in your field and you concentrate on keeping ahead. You encourage Sarah to do the same. She too begins to study, undertaking a course in real estate management. You decide to help her by taking the same course so that you can study together.

You soon settle into the pattern of the upwardly mobile middle class surburban dweller. You borrow money from the finance company for the downpayment on your first house, and work three jobs to make all the different payments. House prices begin to rise and you think it prudent to sell and buy another house to maximise your investment. That causes one of your biggest quarrels and crises.

It is an early summer evening as you are driving Sarah home from work.

"I think we should sell the house and use the proceeds from

the sale to pay down on two houses. We could rent out one and live in the next. If an emergency arose we could easily sell one of them," you say.

"No! If we are going to buy another house I want a new house. We had a lot of trouble cleaning up and repainting the one we are in now."

The previous owner had been a heavy smoker and the smell of the cigarettes has permeated into the woodwork, the curtains, and all parts of the house. It has to be thoroughly cleaned and repainted. Even the floors are refinished. It is a lot of work to get it the way you want.

"I don't intend to inherit anybody else's crosses," she continues. "We have been looking at those houses off Kingston road. I like them."

"But it would be better to get two houses. Think of it as a long-term investment. I can see that in a few years house prices are going to increase again and we could make a nice profit and invest further in real estate." You try to convince her of the economic advantages of your suggestion.

She is adamant.

"I tell you I want a new house. Maybe you can see five years down the road. I can only see what is in front of me. So there is no further argument."

You try again to get her to see your side without avail. In the middle of the day you make arrangements with the real estate agent. You have your home in the suburbs; the fulfilment of the 'American' Dream, in Canada: large house in the suburbs, two-car garage, good job and two jobs to make the payments. Life follows a routine, and the children grow and time passes quickly.

And then everything collapses. The economy stagnates, inflation grows, interest rates increase staggeringly causing some home-owners to walk away from their homes because of difficulty in making mortgage payments. The country is in turmoil. You are not untouched, and your instincts and foresight guide you. Changes in the health care field are on the horizon. You are made redundant from your part-time job, and your mortgage interest rate skyrockets. You realize that drastic measures have to be taken. Fortunately, your work experience and your qualifications are an advantage. Jobs are opening up in the Middle East in your field, and you begin to think of looking in that direction to improve your financial position.

You get brochures on jobs in Saudi Arabia and other Gulf States. You try to discuss the advantages of trying to get a job in one of those places with Sarah. She closes her mind to all of your arguments. But you press on. You apply for a job in Qatar and you are short-listed. When you tell Sarah about this, her reaction is more vehement than you expect:

"If you want to go along, go along, who the hell cares?" That hurts deeply.

You are offered the job. You accept. It is the logical course to take, in your estimation. You rationalize that Sarah will come around to your way of thinking eventually.

She never does.

Life in the Caribbean community in Toronto assumes a Caribbean flavour. Over the years more immigrants from the islands give the city a distinctly different feeling. This city is becoming more cosmopolitan as a liberal immigration policy and the need to increase the population brings other peoples to the city. It becomes warmer as they bring their different customs with them. For the West Indian immigrant, cricket is their lifeblood during those summer days when it is warm enough for this outside activity. Cricket clubs spring up and rivalries grow.

The Match

The annual cricket match between King City and the Toronto Cricket Club was more than a game. It was always an occasion. It was the chance to have an outing like back home. But it was also a struggle. It was like Pickwick against Police, or Spartan against Empire, back home.

It was the chance to get out in the open with friends and family, and meet those whom you had not seen for a long time. It was the chance to be free and uninhibited, to gossip and argue, and be one's self—West Indian—to be with the boys and girls. It was freedom; freedom from winter's cold and its imprisonment. It was the freedom to walk and play in the warmth of the sun. Like back home.

This game was more than a game, it was an event.

The rivalry was like a Barbados versus Trinidad, or West Indies versus England match. Everybody came to the match, for it was a struggle of cultures and peoples, a reliving of history, a struggle of Black and white.

From as early as three o'clock in the morning, chickens would be baking or chicken legs frying. Cakes would be in the oven and sweet breads would be cooling. Pudding and souse and ginger beer and mauby and those things which you couldn't get normally would appear, and later fish cakes would be frying in the buck pot*, at the park. Back home when preparations were being made for an excursion, a number of chickens and ducks would have disappeared from the yard, but here it was easier to get them straight from the supermarket. Somehow supermarket chickens never taste as good as the yard-fowls* back home.

Before the sun appeared, cars would begin to assemble at the club, and coolers, bottles, jugs and all sorts of hard liquor and utensils would be put into car trunks. Those who didn't have cars would crowd into the coaches which had been hired for the trip to King City. By the time they reached King City the whole atmosphere would be West Indian: loud, raucous, happy, accompanied by much arguing, laughing and the feeling that, for this day, they were back home.

This day and this game began like all the other games before. This day Toronto Cricket Club won the toss and decided to bat. Soon the sounds of arguments died down as the battle between bat and ball began. Families had scattered among the trees, and the picnic tables were loaded down with all the goodies. A large number of the men and women, however, were in the club house at the bar drinking, playing dominoes, or arguing.

Mildred, Elaine and a couple of the other domestics were sitting at a table, but unlike most of the others, they were in serious discussion. This in itself was unusual, because serious discussions never took place at these games. The men usually argued about their virility—how many times in one night or day they could go, and for how long, and they made fun of each other's capabilities, or lack thereof.

The women usually indulged in idle gossip, or poking fun at 'how so-and-so dress', or 'who living with who', or 'who just come up'. This group was different. In addition to Mildred and Elaine, there was Dorothy who worked with some rich people in a penthouse apartment on Bloor Street, and Maureen who worked in a government office on Wellesley Street. They were all ambitious and motivated, and were only waiting for their contracts to end to move on and up.

Dorothy was the most vocal of the group, and always voiced strong opinions on most subjects. Today she was holding forth on the 'death trap', as she called it, into which most of the new exiles were falling.

"I don't understand how these idiots can't see what these white bitches are doing to them. All they doing is getting into more debt."

Dorothy didn't like white people. Plain and simple. Every time they met she related stories of her boss and his wife. She didn't like them, she tolerated them. But in their presence she was always smiling, laughing with them, flattering them and giving them the impression that as far as she was concerned, they were the blessed people, God's chosen people.

Her comments to the girls were:

"You alright, I have an objective in view, and if I have to stifle my feelings for a little while, I know how to do dat. I know how to laugh in their face and cuss them in my mind. You think I foolish? Go and cuss them to their face and loss my lil pick? No soul. I know how to get back at them in my own way. An' to besides I only waiting till I get my landed immigrant status to sen' fuh my man. I already tell he dat ef I sen' fuh he he got to married to me in six months time or I going go to the authorities an' pack he ass back, so he better know which side he bread butter pun. I does get lonely as hell lying down in dat attic when de night come, especially in winter and I ent got no human blanket to warm me up."

The other girls listened, enthralled while she recounted an episode which had taken place.

"One time that no-good mistress of mine know dat it was my day off. She know, but she come home drunk, vomit all over the place, and I had to clean it up. The vomit did smell so bad I almost vomit myself. I didn't get downtown til' nearly night-time. I was real pissed off."

"And what you do?" Maureen asked.

"Well, I hold she in my mind and wait for my opportunity. When the chance come, I didn't forget she. I wait good 'til she had a dinner party with all sorts of important guests. When they all finish eating she order me to bring in the coffee. Order mind you, not ask. *Dorothy*, she say, *bring in that coffee now. You know, the special blend that I brought back from Jamaica.* She did only want to show off. *Yes, please Ma'am*, I answer real docile like, *It brew already.* Well, I went in that kitchen and spit in every cup of coffee, and then I stir every cup with my finger. But I won't tell you which finger? Girls you shoulda see me when I bring in that coffee, all smiles, and bowing and giving out the coffee, and *I hope you enjoy your coffee, sir*, and *ma'am, I hope it sweet enough for you.* But deep down inside I saying to myself: Dah fuh lick yuh. If you did only know what you drinking. Bitches! It din' do them nothing but I get satisfaction out of knowing what I do, and *that* they didn't."

Elaine joined in the discussion on the debt trap.

"I agree with Dorothy. Credit too easy to obtain, and our people have not yet learned how to handle it. They see the advertisements: 'no down payment', 'no interest for three months', 'easy terms', and they rush to get credit, and then when the interest payments and other payments become due, they can't handle them."

"That's what I keep saying." Dorothy added in support. "Back home we had to buy everything cash. Your parents drummed into your head that you should avoid debt like the plague. We ent had no history or experience with credit. We din know anything 'bout credit rating. Besides, The Bank wasn't lending Black people money anyhow."

"You right chile," Maureen chimed in, "before I come here I never owe nuhbody nothing. I raise a few stocks an' some chickens to get whatever I wanted. When my father wanted to put on a shed roof on to the li'l two gable house we live in, he buy a few boards every week, and put them under the cellar 'till he had enough. When I come here I find out that you had to go into debt and pay off that debt to get a credit rating. That doesn't make any sense to me."

"And you see what happen now." Dorothy added. "a lot of people in so much debt they spraining their brains how to get out of it. Only the other day Sandra boyfriend get his wages garnish, an' he din' even understand what garnish mean. All he know is that all of a sudden he was working hard as ass, and getting almost nothing to bring home. That never happen to nuhbody back home. Nuhbody ent know nothing 'bout garnishment."

"And annuder thing," Maureen added, "these white people getting on like they do we a favour by employing we as domestic servants. It is people like we who does build up this society. We not the onliest immigrants, all of them is immigrants."

"You damn right!" Dorothy exclaimed, "that mistress of mine come over from Poland, and they din' even have a pot to pee in. They didn't have no chairs nor tables to eat food off of, an now dey get lil position in society, they putting on airs. Back home I had more than them. We had good mahogany furniture in de house."

"But what particularly annoys me," added Elaine, "is that this society as a whole seems to forget that it takes courage and fortitude to come to a place like this to work. Especially when winter sets in. It takes strength and will power to leave all you have known and loved behind, to brave the unknown and start a new life, in many cases subjugating yourself, as Ma used to say, to 'all sorts of humps and grumps', and your pride to reach your goal. It takes a lot out of you emotionally to sever ties with your homeland and adopt a new country, you know how hard it was to leave my child and come here? You know what it is like not to be able to see him, or touch him, or comfort him when he in pain?"

Mildred had been silent all this time listening to the others, but at this point she joined the discussion.

"You know, it would be interesting to have a thorough study of the social impact of immigration on the new country, and the old country, and its effect on the immigrants themselves."

"What do you mean?" Elaine asked.

"Well, take the immigration of the West Indians to England

over the past five to six years. You had a massive influx into that country to help their manpower shortage. A large percentage of them were skilled tradesmen—carpenters, masons, engineers, and intellectuals. The drive to better themselves and their families was the impetus for the immigrants. Although it was voluntary, it was compulsory to some extent, made so by the economic circumstances back home. On the other hand, the sudden loss of skills to the home country must have left a void, and it will take many years to replace them."

"You right girl," Dorothy added, "but I also agree with Elaine, we got to be strong, because if we not strong, the hurt of prejudice and discrimination, the loneliness and the humiliation would drive us all mad."

"Yes," said Mildred, "but what also keeps us going is that invisible umbilical chord which joins us to that little rock we call home. That is the tie that binds."

"But yet some not going back home you know." Maureen added, "I know a few who say they not going back 'causin' back home ent got nutting to offer them, and they couldn't live back there. They ent been back home for years, but they got all sorts of things to say 'bout home and always condemning it."

"That may be true, but you ever notice how they always want news of back home?" Dorothy seemed almost angry as she said it. "I know I going back some day. I don't know when, but it will be someday. I going back home."

"True," said Maureen, "but for a lot of people the time for going back getting put back longer and longer. The new place does take hold of you and you forget 'bout home. When you leave home and come out, you never remain yourself. You become somebody else. You can't get acceptance from the people in the place you come to, and then after a number of years, you can't fit in where you come from. You can't fit in no place. You in purgatory, somewhere between heaven and hell. That is why a lot of people decide not to go back. They got to try to fit in some place. They try to become the same with the new country. They try to talk like them, dress like them, act like them, and live like them. But don't care how they try, they can't become them."

While this discussion was going on, the arguments among the men were getting louder as the games were becoming more exciting. Wickets were quickly falling and it looked as if King City, in their innings, would be bowled out for few runs by the Toronto Club.

Harold went in to bat. As he walked slowly to the wicket, putting on his batting mittens, he thought of the task ahead. Half his side was back in the pavilion, sent reeling by a tall broad-shouldered Pakistani fast bowler who had recently immigrated and become a member of the Toronto Club. It was rumored that he had once played test cricket, but few people had seen him before. He was good. His long run-up to the wicket was smooth, accelerating easily from his mark, delivering the ball from a high trajectory with great speed. He was also skilled in his ability to move the ball both ways off the seam, and through the air. Many of the batsmen he dismissed were not only fooled by the swing of the ball, but had their wicket hit before they were able to get their bats down in time to stop the ball.

Harold reached the wicket and took his guard. He looked around the field at the figure of the fast bowler walking away from him toward his mark, which seemed to be almost half-way to the boundary, at the slip cordon; four slips, a gully, a silly mid-off, a silly mid-on, a short leg, a cover and mid-off, both half-way to the boundary, and a deep mid-wicket. It was a well-placed attacking field. Harold analyzed it. With that type of field setting, he thought, he is going to bowl some out-swingers, looking for the edge of the bat, and some bouncers hoping that I will play the ball to one of the short fielders. He doesn't have a deep mid-off, or a deep square leg, so I'll have to try and get my runs there. He expects me to be defensive, so I'll try to attack. He signaled to the umpire that he wanted to take fresh guard. He shifted closer to the off stump and moved half a step closer to the bowler.

He was ready. There was silence all around the ground. The tap, tap, of his bat on the ground echoed in the still air.

The bowler started his run and approached the wicket with smoothly accelerating speed. He jumped and delivered.

Harold saw a red blur and reacted instinctively, pulling his head out of the way of an extremely fast, vicious bouncer starting slightly outside the line of his off stump, but swinging past his face only to be caught by the wicket-keeper who was standing far back on the leg side. He took a deep breath, twirled his bat, and settled back in his stance to await the next ball.

The red missile left the bowler's hand. Harold watched its flight through the air. Again it was slightly outside the line of the off-stump, but then it suddenly dipped. He again reacted without thought as an in-swinging yorker headed to his stump. He blocked it just in time, stopping it with the bottom of his bat. It almost slipped through. The crowd erupted in applause. They were knowledgeable cricket enthusiasts, who enjoyed a good contest between a good batsman and a good bowler.

He's good, Harold thought, let's see what he is going to bowl next. He didn't have long to wait. The next ball was faster than the previous ones, and landed closer to the line of the center stump, moving away. It was a good out-swinger, but he saw it early and left it alone to be caught by the wicket-keeper, close to the first slip. He played out the rest of the over, getting the ball in the center of his downward sloping bat, and away from any of the close fielders.

He approached his batting partner and they met in the center of the pitch as the fielders changed positions.

"He's fast and good." Harold said.

"I know," John replied, "I don't think I can handle him, so you'll have to try and keep him."

"That's okay. I think I have him figured out. His first three deliveries are extremely fast, but after that he slows down. I don't think his conditioning is very good, so if I can frustrate him for a couple of overs, he will tire and then we can take over. I also watched his run-up. Whenever he is going to bowl the away swinger he delivers it from closer to the stumps. I'll handle him."

John scored a couple of runs, and then it was Harold's turn to face the Pakistani again. His run-up and delivery were as fast as in the previous over. Harold played the first ball easily. He was prepared. As the bowler approached and delivered from close to the stumps, Harold knew it was going to be a fast away-swinger. His bat flashed and the ball was a red blur as it flew between cover and cover-point, hit the boundary board, and rebounded before any of the fielders on the off-side could move. The crowd erupted in loud applause.

Harold was prepared for the bouncer when it came. He rose to his full height and pulled the ball hard and full for six runs over the square leg boundary. The cheering from the spectators was loud and prolonged. He saw what was almost a look of fear in the bowler's eyes. He was not accustomed to this type of treatment by batsmen. When Harold received the next ball, an attempted yorker, he turned it into a full toss by moving a little way down the wicket, and drove it powerfully to the boundary between the mid-off and cover for another four runs. He could tell from the walk of the bowler and the dejected slope of his shoulder that he had won the battle. John approached him and they met in the center of the wicket.

"You don't have to worry about him any more John," Harold said, wiping the perspiration from his forehead. "I've softened him up for you; just play your natural game."

"Okay, let's go from here," John replied, "we can handle them."

They were soon dispatching the ball to all parts of a now very defensively set field. The domino games were equally exciting. The slamming of the dominoes mixed with the comments and arguments made such a din that it was almost necessary to shout in order to be heard.

Elaine went to the bar to get another coke. As she approached a man seated at the bar blocked her path. She tried to move past his leg to go to the other side, but he grabbed her arm. He seemed to be drunk. She looked at him unafraid, and said calmly,

"Please let go of my arm." He didn't release her, but instead tried to bring her to him.

"Oh, come on sweetheart, gimme a lil' kiss." There was a strong smell of alcohol on his breath.

Elaine tried to free her arm again, and said with a little more force and anger:

"I think it would be better for your own good to let go of my arm, and let me get my drink."

Her anger had no effect on him. If anything it seemed to make him more determined. He tried to pull her to him again. The memory of so many years ago came rushing back. This man was white. The slamming of dominoes stopped. The room became deathly still. All eyes turned to Peter, who was seated at the domino table.

Dorothy assessed the situation quickly as she looked in Peter's direction. Alarm spread across her face.

"Oh, Jesus Christ! Oh, JESUS CHRIST! Somebody go an' call Harold quick. Maureen… run fast an' get Harold. He batting. Get he quick or somebody going dead today."

"SHIT!" There was a single exclamation in the stillness of the room.

Maureen understood and ran outside as fast as her legs would carry her onto the cricket field shouting for Harold. She ran right past the fast bowler, right past the umpire, straight to Harold. She spoke to him, agitatedly pointing. Harold dropped the bat and sprinted for the club house. The other players turned and ran also, although they didn't understand what they were running for, or toward.

Harold entered and pushed through the crowd at the door.

Peter was already approaching the man holding Elaine.

"If I was you I would let the little lady go."

Although this was said in a calm, almost quiet voice, each word was like a pistol shot in the quiet room. The man still held Elaine, and everybody seemed frozen in their positions. It was as if they were watching a cobra about to strike.

Elaine looked at Peter and saw the glaze in his eyes. She knew what it meant. She knew, and she was afraid. And Harold knew when he saw it as he entered. He had seen it before. Elaine knew because she had seen it when she had told him about her episode with the overseer.

It was a look which mirrored his feelings. Harold had seen that look at Notting Hill. Other exiles present, many from England, knew of Notting Hill, and had heard of Peter's exploits, and his strength. They knew that this white man in this white man's country was close to death.

Harold sprang between Peter and the man.

"No! No Peter!" he said quietly. "No Peter!"

Peter took another step toward the man and raised his hand.

"No Peter! Please!" Elaine said, looking at him intently. She was hardly breathing. No one seemed to be breathing in the silence.

"Peter, please," Elaine whispered.

Harold held on to Peter's raised hand.

"Peter, it's me, Harold. It's okay. It's okay," he said softly and soothingly.

Meanwhile, the white man's face was pale as a ghost. He released Elaine, and as he did so a number of players from the Toronto Cricket Club with whom he had come, quickly dragged him away. They knew he had come face to face with death.

Elaine held Peter around his waist. Tears were running down her cheeks. Tears of relief, tears of love, tears of tension. Harold still held Peter's hand, but the tenseness had left it. His heart was beating violently. The glaze gradually left Peter's eyes. Elaine led him away to a quiet corner.

"Come honey, let's go and sit down. See, no harm came to me. I'm okay. Harold come with us. Come sweetheart, come and get something to drink. It will calm you down." She turned to Mildred, "Mildred, you come too."

And big, fearsome Peter went quiet as a lamb. He went with the only two people who mattered in the world to him. He went quietly, but everybody knew what he was capable of doing. Elaine knew because he had told her about the events which led to his exile to England.

Back in Barbados, he had almost beaten to death a white man who had kicked a poor Black boy who had tripped and fallen on the man's car, causing a buckle on his school bag to scratch the car. Peter had intervened. It was a natural and spontaneous thing. He was charged with assault with intent, was convicted, reprimanded, and placed on probation. His parents made arrangements for him to go to England. They realized that they had to get him away from the prejudice and rampant discrimination in the island. He had to escape from this place. His sensitivity to injustice would not allow him to survive long before something worse happened. This in itself was ironic, for he was leaving discrimination to go to worse discrimination. He couldn't escape it. Then Notting Hill had occurred.

When she told him about her experiences and her episode with the overseer his love for her made the encounter a personal experience. He swore to her that night as he lay in her arms that he would protect her with his life until he died. She knew he meant it, and she loved him even more.

Now, as she held him in her arms in that quiet corner and gently kissed him, she knew what he had meant. He was as gentle as a lamb with her because he loved her. And even though he was twice as strong as Harold, he listened to him because he loved him also. But with others outside their circle it was different.

The cricket game started again, and the domino games were more subdued. Nobody 'slammed the doms', but Harold did not resume batting—he remained inside with Peter and Elaine until they returned home later that night. Peter hardly spoke for the rest of the evening, and even after they reached their apartment on Shepherd Avenue in Scarborough, he was very quiet.

Elaine fussed over him, and when they eventually went to bed he didn't say much, but just before he fell asleep, he looked at her intently.

"I couldn't let him hurt you. I love you very much."

She held him close to her, and kissed him fiercely. "I know darling, I know, and I love you too."

He fell asleep with his head on her arm, holding her as if he would never let her go. Not that she wanted him to. She loved this bear of a man too much. Even as his soft snores melted in the quiet night, she relived the events of the day, and remembered the time they had met.

It was so simple. One moment she was walking along the icy sidewalk on her way home from shopping at Honest Ed's, and the next she was on her way to the ground. Before she could reach there, however, she was in a pair of arms, and shielded by a huge body. Her shopping was scattered all over the sidewalk, but strong arms were holding her, their owner laughing loudly.

"Little lady," he said putting her on her feet and turning her to face him, "in all my dreams I never thought I would have a beautiful lady fall for me. I know I'm not bad looking, but I can't have women falling for me all over the place like this."

She tried to hide her embarrassment by starting to pick up her packages, but he wouldn't let her. He lifted her off her feet, and placed her on the sidewalk next to the store's plate glass window.

"No, little lady, you wait here. I wouldn't want you to fall again. I'll get them for you. Wait here."

He picked them up, brushing the dirty snow from them, and, going into the store, came out with a large bag to put them all in.

Elaine was touched by his concern, and while he was inside, she looked at him through the window. He was big, with broad shoulders, a narrow waist, and large solid legs. He wasn't very handsome, but the shape of his mouth gave the impression of a constant smile. His eyes, however, drew you to him. They were light brown and sparkled beneath bushy eyebrows, and they seemed to be darting in all directions constantly. They never seemed to be still.

"He's like the doves we have at home," she thought, "they're always looking around for danger."

He came back, and without waiting for her to protest, let her know that he was going right to her door with her, that he wasn't going to let her go falling all over the place, and in addition, that since she had fallen into his arms, it was a sign that he had been chosen to be her protector.

She made a feeble attempt to tell him that she was alright, but it was obvious he wasn't listening. He had made up his mind. Secretly, she felt protected by this gentle giant, for she had felt his gentleness when he put his arm around her to help her across the street car tracks as they went into the Bathurst Street station. They talked about each other's lives until they reached her apartment on Victoria Avenue. He walked her to her door, exchanged phone numbers, and then he was gone with a wave of his hand, promising to call her, and with the laughing comment:

"I'll be here to catch you any time you want to fall."

He was true to his promise.

They became fast friends, and lovers. He became especially excited when she told him about her son back home, and how she was planning to send for him soon. The next day he appeared at her door with a basketball.

"Peter," she asked in surprise, "what are you doing with a basketball?"

"Oh, it's for our son when he comes." He said sheepishly. She was surprised but moved by his assertion that her son was his.

"But he's not coming for a little while yet."

"I know, but all little boys should have a basketball. It will be here when he comes."

She felt like crying.

After that he often brought gifts for a child he had never seen, but had grown to love. Peter was wonderful. It was only when she told him of her experiences with the overseer at the plantation that she saw the anger in his eyes, she saw them darken and glaze over and realized the depth of his feelings. When the moment passed, however, he calmed down and tears came to his eyes. She knew then how much he loved her.

This day when he had almost killed to protect her, tears fell from her eyes onto his forehead, as she hugged him to her breast and she knew the depth of her own feelings for him.

PART VI

Home

Fini

It is the year of the beginning, or the year of the ending. It is the beginning of the year when it starts, and it is the end of the year when it ends. It is the end of a year when you realize it, although it may have started at the beginning of that year. But now it is the end of an era. You are starting anew, and so is your 'home'.

Canada is undergoing a transition. It is changing. Everything is changing, everybody is changing. It is not the same as it was when you became an exile. The era of the 'philosopher king' ends, and the innocence of the country is being overtaken by the reality of austerity.

As the plane starts its descent you look out of the window at that green oasis in the ocean and know that you have returned home forever. Hours before when you had left your 'home', your mind had been in turmoil.

You settle into your seat, and through the maelstrom of emotions and feelings rising in intensity with the increasing whine of the engines, you go back to that time, to the occasion when you told your friends of your decision to return home.

******

You were sitting in the new mall on Yonge Street one evening sipping coffee in your favorite restaurant, deep in thought, when Harold arrived. He touched you lightly on your shoulders.

"You look as if you are a thousand miles from here."

"Yes Harold," You replied, "I am more than a thousand, I am three thousand, I'm back home in Bim. I'm going back home."

"What are you talking about?" he answered with surprise, "Why would you want to go home? You have a home here. You have everything. You're a Canadian citizen, you have achieved the American dream; beautiful house in the suburbs, two cars in the garage, a good job, academic achievements, and you are popular with your co-workers and friends."

"Yes," You answered, "but I'm not happy."

"Oh come on now, you have everything to make you happy. Your wife loves you and I'm sure that..."

"No Harold," You interrupted, "that's not really true. Our life has been a lie for the last couple of years. She doesn't love me, if she ever did."

Harold was really concerned. He was conscious of your hurt and tried to comfort you.

"Tell me about it. Start at the beginning. I'm a good listener."

You and Harold had become very good friends over the years, and he was easy to talk to.

"I am really perplexed," he said, "because you were such an inspiration to Mildred and me. We saw your ambition and drive, and it stimulated us to achieve. I am due to graduate from university soon and Mildred will get her degree in Business Administration at the same time. We owe it all to your inspiration, encouragement, and support."

You were flattered, for you knew how hard they had worked. As soon as Mildred's contract as a domestic servant was ended, she moved in with Harold. They got married in a quiet wedding at City Hall. Peter was the best-man. You, Sarah, Elaine, and a couple of the other domestics were the only guests at the reception. It was a nice quiet affair, like the nice quiet couple whose wedding it was. Her family came up for the occasion.

Over the years her relationship with her father had improved. She had kept in close contact with them, spending large sums of money on telephone calls, but it was worth it. Her father softened his attitude and wrote her long letters, seeking her understanding. She wrote equally long ones telling him of events in her life and outlining her plans. She was ecstatic when he told her he would come to the wedding and 'give her away'. He would have liked his mother and Joe, his mentor, to have come, but Joe was getting on in age and neither he nor Harold's mother wanted to travel. They let him know that he had their blessings though.

It was a lovely wedding. Her father was very emotional in his speech, and had to wipe away a few tears. Her mother held his hands tightly, showing her deep love and affection for him, and Mildred loved him more than she knew how to say.

She and Harold soon settled into the routine of work and study similar to the pattern of your own life. All of you had become very close over the years, and talked and dreamed your dreams together.

The memories came back and the words flowed easily and naturally as you recalled the events which led up to this moment.

"You know, maybe my mistake was working too hard to achieve my dreams. Maybe I reached them too quickly. Maybe it was my dream, and I took it for granted that it was also her dream. Maybe I assumed that she would understand. But now that I look back on it, maybe I shouldn't have worked so hard."

"But how else could you have achieved it?" Harold asked. "You started with nothing."

"Yes I know, but maybe because I started with nothing, and achieved so much in such a short time, a lot of people who were envious probably influenced her the wrong way. So instead of supporting me when I needed that support, it was not forthcoming, and I had to work harder than might have been necessary."

"I don't know if that is true," Harold answered sort of defensively, "your wife was always a good home maker, a good cook, and a good mother."

"Yes, but she never seemed to be able to understand my objectives. Remember when we sold our first house?"

"I remember that quite well," Harold said, "I especially remember, because when you told me how you had been able to obtain it without any money of your own, I told Mildred about it. She felt, however, that the price you paid in terms of the physical and mental stress was too high."

"I know. Even now when I look back on it, I think I must have been a bit crazy to have done it. I mean, to borrow money from the finance company for the down-payment, then to obtain a mortgage, and then to borrow more money for furniture. It meant that I had to work three jobs to meet those payments."

"We wondered how you didn't collapse, because you were also finishing your thesis at the same time. How did you manage? Even today we can't understand how you did it."

"With great difficulty, stamina, and stick-to-it-ness, plus the fear of what would happen if I ever got sick for any length of time." You tried to be flippant, but the words didn't suit the moment. "When house prices started to rise soon after we bought that first house, I thought it wise to sell ours, make a profit, and invest in two houses. That's where the trouble started. She wanted to live in a big new house, in a new subdivision. She didn't want to live in another second-hand house. As she said, she didn't want to "inherit anybody's crosses". We argued about it for a long time. I couldn't get her to see the economic advantage, in the long term, of investing in two houses. I eventually gave in, and so we got our new house, in a new subdivision."

"But you must admit," Harold interjected, "it is a very nice house: four bedrooms, backyard big enough to carry a swimming pool, and a large lot. We've had a lot of fun there over the years. That's why I can't understand why you are thinking of leaving it."

"Because, I'm not happy." You answered. "I can't stay where I'm not happy, and I'm not made to feel welcome in my own home. Do you know what it is to feel like an exile when you enter your door? Do you know what it feels like to have loved completely, and then realize that the one you love has no affection for you? Can you imagine what it is like to live in your own house and not know the warmth of love? No Harold, I can't take it any more. I have to leave."

"But why did you let it reach this stage? Why didn't you let us help you? We are your friends. Aren't we?" He looked at you intently, seeking assurance.

"Of course you are. But you know I have always been a private person. I always tried to solve my problems alone, in my own way. I didn't like to bother people. I figured they have their own problems."

"You were always helping other people with theirs."

There was a hint of anger in his voice.

"Why didn't you think you could call on some of these same people for help? Look how many times you helped Mildred and me. You kept us together in difficult times. You did the same for Elaine and Peter, and now you are a very important part of our lives. Your concern strengthened the bond between us. We would have done the same for you."

"I know," you answered lamely, "but maybe it's a major fault in my personality. I always want to keep my feelings and my hurt inside. Keep them hidden."

There was a momentary silence between the two of you.

"Do you know, I thought of killing myself?" You said, quietly. "I almost did. I actually attempted to."

Harold looked at you, shock and amazement showing on his face.

"I don't believe you," he said, "No, not you. What would or

could have caused you to think of something like that?"

"Actually, I thought of it twice. Once after we had a violent quarrel over something I had forgotten to do. She told me some things which hurt me pretty bad. She was not sleeping with me at the time. She had moved into one of the other rooms. My stepchildren had grown up and left home, so it was only the two of us in that big house. I was so hurt, so despondent, and I was feeling so alone, that after she had gone to bed, I got up, dressed, got in my car and drove to the railroad tracks near by the lake. I stopped the car across the tracks and just sat in the car with my eyes closed, waiting for God and the train."

"My God!" Harold exclaimed, "Is this really true?"

His knuckles showed the tightness of his grip on his coffee cup.

"Oh yes, it's true. I've never told this to anybody before. It was quite late, about two in the morning. But I guess God wasn't ready for me. For some unknown reason the train broke down that night. It never came. After a while sitting there, I started the car and drove back home. And for a moment, before I fell asleep, I thought, *isn't it funny? Nobody wants me, not even God.*"

"Oh sweet Jesus." Harold was clearly worried. He sat in silence for a while. "What happened after that?" he inquired.

"Things got worse between us. Nothing I did seemed to please her. I bought her flowers, gifts, I did everything to show her how much I loved her, but it didn't help. Then the economic downturn struck the whole country. Do you remember that time?"

"Oh yes, I remember it quite well," Harold replied, "People were losing their homes all over the place. Interest rates shot straight up, and many people just couldn't keep up their payments. Fortunately, because of Mildred's business sense and your advice, we were able to secure a nice little home. See how important you are to us? You can't leave us and go back. We all have an interest in you. Have you told Peter and Elaine yet?"

"No I haven't," you replied. "I've been trying to figure out how to do it, especially now that Elaine's son has joined them. Peter has become like a father to him, and adores him. They remind me so much of what it was like when I first came here."

You were silent for a while with the memories of those early days, those happy days, those days when your feelings, your emotions, your love, were like the roses bursting into bloom after the snows had melted, and the rains of spring had washed the slush away. When the warm summer sun had coaxed them into opening their petals to let their perfume sweeten the air. When the wind in return gave vent to its own feelings by blowing warm and sweet over the landscape. Those were the happy early days of marriage; the middle years of exile.

You brought your thoughts back to the reality of the moment and continued your narrative.

"From the time that crisis started I could see what was happening to the country, the hospital where I was working, and what it was going to be like later on. I applied for a job in the Middle East and got it. I saw this as a way out of our economic difficulties. I hoped it would help solve our emotional problems. Of course I rationalized wrong, because I thought that if I went away, and then she joined me, we would be alone together, away from any influences, and we could work things out. It didn't turn out that way."

"Why not?" His question was direct.

"I would give a thousand dollars if I could find out. You can never imagine the hours I've spent going over every event in our lives to see where I went wrong. Do you know that even when I got that job overseas, it didn't seem to matter to her if I went or if I stayed? I was heart-broken by her attitude, but I still loved her."

Harold looked at his watch and looked around the mall.

"Do you have to leave?" You asked apprehensively. You

didn't want him to leave, he had become your therapist. You needed his presence and his ear for your therapy.

"No, I don't have to leave, and even if I did, I wouldn't leave you at this time. I am supposed to meet Mildred, so I was looking for her."

"Would you like another cup of coffee?" You asked.

"No," he answered, "I'd prefer a rum and coke. What you are telling me requires stronger stuff to settle my nerves."

You called the waiter over, ordered rum and coke for Harold and another cup of coffee. You continued.

"By the time I left home for Qatar, I was a nervous wreck. Leaving was the most painful moment of my life, although I tried not to show it."

Consternation registered in Harold's face. He was about to speak when Mildred came to the table. She put her arms around him and kissed him.

"Hello darling," she said to Harold, "I was looking all over for you. Why didn't you meet me by Eaton's as you promised?"

"Sorry sweetheart," he said, "but I was here talking and never got there." The tone of his voice told her that something was wrong, and when she saw the look on his face, she realized that she was right.

"Harold, what's wrong? What's the matter?"

"I'm going back home," you answered before Harold could say anything.

She sat down abruptly.

"For good?" It was as if the words had not fully registered. "You're leaving for good?"

"Yes, I've made up my mind to return home."

She looked at Harold.

"Can't you make him change his mind Harold? What happened to make him come to this sudden decision?"

"It's not a sudden decision. I've been thinking about it for a couple of months." You answered.

"But why? What's the reason? I thought you were happy

here with us, with everything."

"It seems that a lot of things were going on in his life that we didn't know about. He's been filling me in, and that is why I didn't meet you."

There was genuine concern on her face.

"You mean a lot to us," she said, looking at you intently. "We will miss you, really miss you." There was no doubting the sincerity in her voice.

"I know, but this is a decision that had to be made. I have to do it for my sanity, and maybe to maintain my nature as a law abiding citizen."

Tears were coming close to the surface. You didn't want them to reach there.

"Here let me get you something to drink." You interrupted, "Would you like a rum and coke? Harold I'll get you another one. Fill her in till I get back."

You were glad for the respite away from them. The tears were really close. As you waited for the drinks at the bar, you saw their reflection in the mirror, and saw Mildred wipe her eyes as Harold talked to her earnestly.

You returned with the drinks and as you set them on the table she reached out and covered your hand with hers. Harold too reached out and put his hand over hers and yours. In that wordless moment you knew their love, and knew that they understood your feelings.

Mildred took a sip of her drink and asked you to continue.

"I arrived in Doha, the capital of Qatar," I said, remembering the excitement I felt as I approached the new country, "I had been appointed a supervisor at the new hospital. As the plane came in for the landing it passed over a white pyramid shaped building whose beauty struck me immediately. It was the first of many new, beautiful, and sometimes, shocking events which provided me with another perspective in my life. That beautiful building turned out to be the hotel where I would be housed for a while, until I was given my own villa. That year and a half gave me a greater insight into human nature. I found the Arabs to be warm and friendly, but the nature of the society, its adherence to Islamic doctrine, and the disparity between the wealth of the natives and the poverty of the immigrant laborers from other countries, as well as the social stratification based on status provided me with a lifetime of experience."

"We couldn't understand why your wife didn't go with you," Mildred said, reaching over to touch Harold. "I know that if Harold went anywhere to work, I would go with him."

They kissed and linked fingers.

"I wanted her to, and she actually came for a couple of weeks of her vacation from work," you answered defensively, "but I guess that the difference in cultures, the absence of her friends and other things may have influenced her against it. Maybe the sacrifice would have been too much."

"It's no sacrifice." Mildred was adamant. "It's no sacrifice to be with the one you love. To my mind marriage should be an act of trust in the good sense and intentions of your partner. I trust Harold's motives and his intentions." He put his arm around her and brought her closer to him.

"There was one event which made a lasting impression on me, in a sort of negative way, and when my contract ended I was not too interested in renewing it."

"What was it?" Harold asked with curiosity.

"It concerned a horse, an ordinary-looking sick horse. As I passed on my way to work one morning he was standing outside the high wall of the building. As he took a limping step forward the sores on his leg and rump were evident. Then he stood there looking around, and in his eyes, which once must have been soft, there was the cloudiness of pain. Later when I returned home he was still there. He seemed not to have moved the entire day, even though the temperature must have reached at least 110 degrees. There was no shade anywhere. The sky was blue and cloudless. There was no wind. I missed him the next day. He was nowhere around, or at least I did not see him when I passed.

The following day however, I saw the reason why I had not seen him the day before. He was lying on the ground next to the pile of sand the workmen were using to prepare the mortar for the houses they were building. There he was, between the cement mixer, the sand and the cement blocks. At first I thought he was dead, but then he painfully raised his head. And the workmen passed him by. They worked around him. All day he lay there, and the temperature rose, and there was no shade. And the workmen worked around him. The next day he was still there. Again I thought he was dead, but the legs moved, and he still tried to lift his head. And no one did anything. He was dying, but still they worked around him.

As I passed to and fro on the way to work, I wondered why no one did anything. Why didn't I do anything? Every day I passed the veterinary hospital on my way to work. I wanted to do something, but I didn't. Had I become so uncaring?

The next day I stopped. The man at the gate approached. In a small shed in the yard they were clipping the hooves of a goat. I gave the traditional greeting, *Salaam alakum.* He replied: *Alakum a Salaam.* I said: *Ana batkalin inglese bas,* which means: I only speak English. I had learned the few words of Arabic which allowed me to indicate my inability to converse freely in the language. He asked: *Enta batkalin Arabi?*—do you speak Arabic? I replied: *La batkalin Inglese, maafi Arabi*—No I don't speak Arabic, only English.

There is a horse, I tried to show by signs what I was speaking about, which is sick.

He answered in English, where?

Near where I live, just up the road. He is sick and dying.

So what do you want?

I wanted to tell someone who would go to see him.

You know who he belongs to?

No.

Well, maleesh. Forget it.

He turned back to the goat. I left.

When I passed the next day the horse did not move his head this time. The marks on the ground showed where the tractor had removed the body. The workmen continued building the house."

There were tears in Mildred's eyes. She loved animals, and the thought of the animal's suffering was more than she could accept.

"How cruel!" she exclaimed.

"It might appear to be cruel, but that is a harsh area, a harsh climate, conditions and living. There can be no sympathy for the sick, weak or dying. Death is accepted as an integral part of living. Death is inevitable for the living. Every breath we breathe, and every day we live brings us closer to the death that exists with life."

A huge hand suddenly descended on your shoulder. You instinctively knew who it was.

"Peter!" You exclaimed. "How are you?"

You looked up and into Peter's eyes. There was anger in them.

"Shite man," he said loudly, "I thought we were good enough friends that you would at least tell us you were leaving." He turned to Harold and Mildred.

"Did you know he was going back home?" he asked, as if they were also conspirators in the cover-up.

"No," Harold answered, "we are now hearing it for the first time."

Peter tightened his grip on your shoulder and kept you pinned to the chair as you tried to rise.

"Elaine home crying. She got the news from her friend at the travel agency. I don't like nobody to make Elaine cry." He said it emphatically.

"Its okay Peter," Harold interjected, "he's now telling us the reason why. Sit down and join us." Peter released his grip, and sat at the table still grumbling,

"Elaine home crying."

"Another event happened which made me realize that I was no longer wanted," you continued, "and even though I tried for months for a reconciliation, I finally had to admit that it was really all over. After that I made my decision. Canada, my home, was no longer home. It no longer held anything for me. I certainly didn't need to struggle any longer in those long cold winters. It had served its purpose. I had served my purpose. It was time to go home. It was time to escape, like that first time, so many years ago."

The four of you sat there for a long time after you finished your narrative, silent, immersed in your own thoughts. When you finally parted in the late fall evening, agreeing to meet for one last time, you all embraced warmly.

You met with them one last time for dinner before you left for your island home. You arrived early at the revolving restaurant atop the Harbour Castle Hilton, on the Harbour-front. You had chosen this place because it rekindled memories of pleasant dinners on the occasions of Valentine's, birthdays, or other celebrations of happier times. It also provided a panoramic view of the city, the islands, and the suburbs—a view you wanted to imprint on your memory, for it would have to last the rest of your life.

It was not yet dark when they arrived together. As usual, Elaine and Mildred were dressed in stunning outfits, and looked as lovely as you had ever remembered. Everyone in the restaurant seemed to be looking at them admiringly.

Peter and Harold had to intervene in their light-hearted competition for the right to sit next to you. It was finally agreed that Mildred would sit next to you and Elaine across from you, next to the window. Peter and Harold kept guard on the outer seats.

As the restaurant turned, giving a view of the city, you visualized all those places which were so familiar—University

Avenue, where you worked, and Yonge Street, the pulsing aorta of this growing city, and off in the distance, the East End and the Borough of Scarborough, which had been your home for so long. With a start you realized that Elaine was speaking to you.

"Promise us you'll write often. Keep us informed of all that's happening, and how you're doing. If things don't work out, come right back, you are always welcome to stay with us."

"If he doesn't, I will personally go down to Bim and throttle him." Peter interjected, light-heartedly demonstrating how he would do it.

"What I want more than anything is for him to stay." Mildred added. "I still don't see why he has to go back."

There was a lump in your throat, and you welcomed the intervention of the waiter bringing the drinks.

"Mildred…" you spoke with difficulty. "…I love all of you, you are all very dear to me, and if I felt there was any other way I wouldn't go, but I need time. I need time to myself, time for peace and tranquility, time to settle this turmoil in my mind, time to get my head back together again. I have to return because it is only in the peace and tranquility of my homeland that I can maintain my sanity. I love this country, but it is not home. The wind here is cold, and I hear the warm wind calling. I'm tired of being an exile. I'm tired of the cold, I'm tired of this rat race, I'm tired of this struggle which has been a journey to reach the cup at the top of the mountain—that shining cup, that Holy Grail, which holds the drink of eternal happiness, but having climbed the mountain, and reached the cup, the drink is bitter like wormwood. Like the drink they gave Our Savior on that other mountain, and having tasted it, I wonder whether the struggle was worth the effort. Right now I am tired and exhausted, mentally and physically. Please try to understand."

Harold looked at you intently.

"I understand fully what you are feeling. I know the feelings of the exile. I know the longing and the loneliness. Fortunately I have Mildred to comfort me at those times. You'll be okay when you get back. You are psychologically ready to return. Many exiles return before they are ready, suffer from culture shock, and are unhappy when the country does not conform to their expectations. Then they come back to the same thing they want to escape from. They can't find that happiness they seek."

The waiter came with the food and conversation ceased for a short while. Peter was unusually contemplative, and hardly touched his meal. Elaine looked at him with concern.

"Peter, honey, what's bothering you? You're not eating much."

He was pushing peas around the plate with his fork, and seemed to be far away in his thoughts.

"I was just wondering whether all this sacrifice is worth it. I can see all my friends back home, going to fetes, having beach parties, enjoying life. All we seem to be doing is battling with snow, ice, and cold weather, fighting prejudice at all corners, having to be on guard all the time. I wonder if it's worth it. I have not been home in such a long time." He looked at Elaine seeking assurance.

"Yes darling, it's worth it." She pulled him close to her. "If we had never come here, I would not have met you, and you are the most wonderful person I ever met. You've made me feel loved and protected. Yes darling, despite everything, it's worth it." She hugged him fiercely.

"I agree with Elaine," Mildred added, "by leaving home, we have had opportunities we could never get. We have had the chance to achieve our dreams, and, although it is difficult, we have a lot to be thankful for. Now, on another note, I have an announcement to make." She looked at Harold, and pulled him close. "I want all of you to know. We are going to have a baby."

"What?" Peter exclaimed loudly. There was an immediate

change in his demeanor. He loved children.

"Yes," Mildred reiterated, "Harold and I are going to have a baby. I was only waiting for the right occasion to let all of you know."

"Well in that case, I might as well let everybody know that I am pregnant," Elaine announced a wide, mischievous, smile on her lips.

"What?" Peter's shout was even louder this time. He was ecstatic. He jumped on the seat and announced to everyone in the restaurant:

"We're pregnant! I mean, my wife's pregnant! We're going to have babies! I mean we're going to have a baby!"

Elaine was having difficulty calming him down and getting him to sit, but his excitement was infectious. All the patrons in the restaurant cheered loudly. The manager sent over a magnum of champagne, and there was toasting and clinking of glasses all around. Mildred and Elaine hugged each other, and immediately began talking about babies, excluding the men.

The night ended on a high note as the realization of the new paths ahead for the group became clear. Changes were taking place in your lives. For you the circle was complete, you had completed your journey, your odyssey. For them a new phase was on the horizon. They represented a new Canada, a changing country, a new beginning.

The day for your departure finally came. They were heartbroken when you said goodbye at the airport, and as you embraced them you knew that they too were wondering about the day when they too would be going home.

Before that, though, they had to fulfill some part of their destinies in this 'home'. They had succeeded to this point, and although they were from diverse backgrounds, brought together by adversity, they were now a unit, providing each other with the strengths, the will and the desire to succeed even further.

******

It is snowing lightly as the plane lifts off the tarmac, snowing like the night when you first landed here, and as it banks on its way south you look outside at the lines of rushing vehicles and twinkling lights, and realize with sadness that you are leaving part of yourself behind. You close your eyes as a tear courses its way down your cheek. Something tugs at your heartstrings and a feeling akin to that you first experienced when you left to go to Harpur comes over you. This time, however, there is no question to ask about the time of your return. You are going home.

Home!

You soon drift off into merciful sleep.

The plane lands smoothly, and taxies up to the ramp. The other returning nationals, like you, cheer loudly. They too are home. You descend the steep steps and look at the new terminal. You feel the warm breeze blowing across the tarmac, whispering its words of welcome.

As you enter the hall and move into the line for 'returning residents and citizens', the bright smile of the female immigration officer dressed in her smart brown and white uniform welcomes you back home, and you know you are no longer an exile.

Epilogue

Now you sit on this rock,
and quietly talk to the wind;
the wind
which listens,
and the waves
which wash your feet,
and the sun
which warms your skin.
And you listen as the trees whisper
with their leaves,
and the ocean's deep, sonorous, voice
is the background
to the music of the birds
which fills your soul with joy,
and you are at peace.
Home.

Glossary

[The] Bank

    Barclays Bank, the only major bank existing in the island at that time

Big-botsy

    Referring to a woman with a large bottom

Bubbies

    Breasts

Buck-pot

    A cast iron skillet, similar to the Dutch oven, used for frying

Buller

    A homosexual

Bum knock and spree

    A party, fete, dance or any entertainment that was taking place

Bus stand cabinet

    A group of people who congregated in the bus stand every night to discuss and argue boisterously about current political topics

Chattel house

    A small wooden house of unique design which could be easily dismantled, transported on a cart and reconstructed in a short time

Clammy Cherry

    A vine like shrub whose seeds are surrounded by a gummy sap

Clap

    Gonorrhea, a sexually transmitted disease

Cou-cou stick

A small bat-shaped piece of wood used to stir cornmeal mixed with okra to the consistency required, in preparing cou-cou, a local dish. Cou-cou is similar to fou-fou a dish brought over from Africa by slaves, usually made from crushed yam or manioc

Crocus bag

A bag made of jute which was used to transport sugar

Cut-eye

A look of derision or contempt

Domestic scheme

An arrangement between the Barbados and Canadian governments which provided employment opportunities for young women to go to Canada to work as domestic servants on contract. After fulfillment of their contracts, they had the opportunity to be granted landed immigrant status in Canada

Empire Day

A holiday celebrated by British colonies celebrating the jubilee of Queen Victoria

Exhibition

The annual agricultural fair and exhibition of produce, animals goods, crafts and everything related to agriculture. The tradition was for everyone who attended to wear their finest, it was the "coming out" occasion for young men and women, and it provided an outlet and opportunity for persons from the country to come to town

[The] Federation

Refers to the short-lived West Indian Federation which was disbanded following a referendum put to the people of Jamaica recommmending withdrawal, which they accepted

Fire-rage

To take on someone else's quarrel [take up fire-rage for someone]

Foop

Sexual intercourse

Fowl coop

Cage for domestic fowls which almost all families kept

Fray cakes

Small fish (frays), usually netted near the beach, which are mixed in a batter of flour and spices and dropped into a pan of hot oil and fried

Front house

The 'living room' or 'drawing room' of a chattel house

Grunt

A small fish usually found near the shore

High Collar shirt jac

A style of dress first adopted by males soon after independence. It was a short-lived attempt to change formal attire from the jacket and tie required for formal dress

Horning

Cuckolding, infidelity, the process of being unfaithful to your partner

Jalousies

Wooden slats placed in the door or window of a chattel house which could be opened to let in air or closed to keep out the rain

Jerk-waist

A form of dance in which the waist was jerked up and down on each side to the rhythm that was being played

Lady Boat

A Canadian freighter trading between Canada and the West Indies. These freighters all have names of British heroes, such as 'Lady Drake' and 'Lady Nelson'.

Lead-pipe

A small sweet bread made with coconut

Lighter

Thirty- or forty-foot long boats designed to hold cargo. These 'freighters' were propelled by eight- to ten-foot oars, each pulled by a single 'lighter man'. All cargo was brought to shore by these lighters

Lighter-man

A labourer who worked on the lighters pulling the long oars that propelled the vessel

Lime

To stand on the sidewalk and pass the time of day just observing passers-by and fraternizing

[The] Little Eight

Referred to the number of West Indian islands left after the withdrawal of Jamaica and later Trinidad from the West Indies Federation

Little England

The name given to Barbados because of its close ties and adoption of many of the english customs

Loopy-dog

A dog who slinks away with his tail between his legs

Maiden

Refers to a girl's virginity

Magic Lantern

A manually operated slide projector which projected painted colour images onto a screen. The images and descriptions were etched on glass slides

Morris chair

A particular type of chair, usually made of mahogany, with a semicircular back and cane bottom

Pint-and-a-half bottle

A bottle holding roughly 150 ml. of liquid

[The] pipe

The communal pipe in the village where each household collected their water for drinking and household requirements. There was no running water in individual households normally, only the more affluent could afford this. Quite often some people, instead of waiting in line, tried to push their buckets ahead of the person in front with the inevitable result of a 'stand-pipe fight'. Much of the village gossip and news usually took place at the stand-pipe, or the 'pipe'

[The] Pit

The first eight or nine rows in the movie theatre. These were the cheapest seats in the cinema and were thus the ones occupied by the poorest and roughest patrons

Poor bakra johnny

A corruption of 'poor back row johnny'; usually associated with the poor whites who were descendents of indentured servants brought over from Scotland or Ireland to work in the fields. When they went to church they were usually given places 'in the back rows' of the church

Red Legs

The indentured servants brought over to work in the fields. Their legs usually got sun burnt, thus the term 'red legs'

Rock hind

A small bottom-dwelling fish

Sea-cat

Octopus

[The] Shed

A building near Queens Park which was the venue for many dances and social hops

Shed roof

An addition to the back of the chattel house, usually housing the kitchen and a small dining area

Social-hop

Dances held to raise funds. They were held in small halls or even homes. An admission charge was levied and the money was collected at the door and usually kept in a small suitcase in the custody of the person keeping the social hop

Spaugie

Emaciated

Spider

A hand-drawn cart specially designed to carry puncheons of molasses

Spouge

A uniquely Barbadian musical rhythm and beat introduced

and popularized by Jackie Opel, one of the island's foremost, singers and stage performers of the late sixties

Star apple tree

A tall tree bearing a small tasty fruit with a soft interior similar to that of the kiwi fruit.

Stuff cart

A cart used to collect and transport garbage

Sweeps

Long oars about eight to ten feet in length used to propel the lighters of cargo

Trash house

A building in Queens Park with a roof of palm fronds

Thinking Day

The annual occasion for all Boy Scout troops in the island to gather, parade and renew their pledges to the Scout Movement

[The] Under Forties

A group of young Barbadians (all under forty years of age) who campaigned for Barbados to enter a federation with the 'little eight' rather than seek independence alone

West Indies Federation

The single occasion when all the West Indian Islands formed a Federation

Whomper

A machete or cutlass. Also referred to as a 'Collins'

Woman Tongue Tree

Sometimes called a shack-shack tree. The dried seed pods hanging on the tree keep up a constant 'chatter' in the wind and never seem to stop

Wukking up

Gyrations to rhythm and drumming involving sexually suggestive motions of the hips

Yard-fowl

Chickens raised in the yards of households. It may also refer to a person who follows and rigorously defends a political party at all costs

Zapatas

Sandals whose soles were made of rubber, usually cut from a car tyre, with straps of multi-coloured woven cotton

ABOUT THE AUTHOR

Alvin Cummins has been writing seriously since 1985 and is inspired primarily by Barbadians and Barbadian situations.

Cummins was born in Barbados and has lived, studied and worked in Jamaica, New York, Toronto and Doha Qatar in the Arabian Gulf. He recently completed his studies leading to an M.Phil. in Microbiology. He has also been an actor on stage and in television and radio dramas.

He is the writer of a number or literary works in various genres: four plays (*The Homecoming, Three Women, I-Jah,* and *Jaja King of Opobo*); three musicals: (*East Side-West Side, Emmerton,* and *Redemption*); and novels: (*The Wind Also Listens,* and *The Royal Palms Are Dying*).

ALSO BY ALVIN CUMMINS

For over three hundred years the island of Barbados has been a model of stability. This stability is due in no small measure to the upstanding mores, values, adherence to the law and respect for these laws, the law-givers and those in authority. Politicians, teachers, police and the administration have been The Royal Palms—straight, clean, upright and upstanding—which have held the fabric of the society together.

Unfortunately, a lack of integrity and an abandonment of the precepts that formed the foundation of the society have been adversely influenced by outside forces which, like termites, have brought about the dangerous demise of its stability.

In this work Cummins has chosen the theme of the 'Royal Palms' because he sees a loss of the values in the Barbadian society at this time resulting in the loss of the "stateliness" of the island and its people.

LaVergne, TN USA
22 December 2009
167769LV00001B/6/P